Marriage vs. Single Life:
How Science and the Media Got It So Wrong

Bella DePaulo, Ph.D.

ISBN: 150588635X
ISBN-13: 978-1505886351

Also by BELLA DePAULO

Singled Out: How Singles Are Stereotyped, Stigmatized, and Ignored, and Still Live Happily Ever After

The Science of Marriage: What We Know That Just Isn't So

The Best of Single Life

Singlism: What It Is, Why It Matters, and How to Stop It

Single with Attitude:
Not Your Typical Take on Health and Happiness, Love and Money, Marriage and Friendship

Behind the Door of Deceit:
Understanding the Biggest Liars in Our Lives

The Hows and Whys of Lies

When the Truth Hurts: Lying to Be Kind

The Lies We Tell and the Clues We Miss: Professional Papers

Is Anyone Really Good at Detecting Lies? Professional Papers

Friendsight: What Friends Know that Others Don't

New Directions in Helping: Volumes 1, 2, and 3

The Psychology of Dexter

How We Live Now:
Redesigning Home and Family in the 21st Century
(forthcoming, August 2015)

CONTENTS

PART IV: WHAT'S REALLY GOING ON HERE?

Preface

Hardly a week goes by without a media report of the latest research on marriage. Reporters want click bait and they seem to think they can find it in studies proclaiming that getting married transforms miserable and sickly single people into happy and healthy couples. Decades ago, when my own research focused almost exclusively on the psychology of lying and detecting lies, I didn't pay much attention to those claims. But then I decided to devote my research and writing to single life, and I began to read the original research reports very closely.

I was stunned by what I found. Many of those studies – the ones described as showing that getting married makes people happier or healthier or better off in some other psychological or interpersonal way – did nothing of the sort. Methodologically, too many were just embarrassingly bad. There are some good ones, but look closely at the findings, and you will see that they do not support the blanket claims that have been made about the benefits of getting married. In fact, in some studies, it is the people who stay single, and not those who marry, who fare best.

You'd never know that from the claims that are made, not just by reporters and pundits, but even by our most celebrated social scientists and authors, such as Dan Gilbert and Dan Buettner. Influential judicial decisions cite claims that getting married makes people happier and healthier. Countless programs, organizations, books, and opinion pieces take those claims as truths. But they are not true.

I have been trying to make that case for nearly two decades. As a social scientist, I care about the accuracy of claims about research findings. But when it comes to proclamations about marriage and single life, the issues are not just academic. Real single people – over 100 million of them in the U.S. alone – are getting the message that science has shown that their lives are second rate. It hasn't and they aren't.

In the past few years, several important studies and review papers have been published that make it clearer than it has ever been before that we have been misled about the supposed benefits of getting married. I have discussed those publications in several of the brief chapters in this book, many of which were posts that first appeared on my "Living Single" blog at *Psychology Today* or my "Single at Heart" blog at *Psych Central*.

The most important chapter, I think, is Chapter 2, "No study has ever shown that getting married makes people happier or healthier – and no study ever will." In it, I make the case more thoroughly and forcefully than ever before. In fact, I think that chapter is so significant that I have published it as a stand-alone book, *The Science of Marriage: What We Know That Just Isn't So*.

The first chapter in this book, "Living single: Lightening up those dark, dopey myths," is a broad-ranging discussion of the psychology of single life. In it, I challenge the pervasive claims about the benefits of marriage, but that is just a part of the discussion. The chapter originally appeared in Cupach and Spitzer's edited volume, *The Dark Side of Personal Relationships II*. As with most academic volumes, it is very expensive. Now interested readers can access my chapter in this much more affordable book.

Part I of *Marriage vs. Single Life: How Science and the Media Got It So Wrong* includes just those two substantial chapters. The second chapter was originally written for fellow academics and some sections are fairly detailed.

Part II begins with Chapter 3, a briefer and more accessible version of the same arguments from Chapter 2. The chapters, 3 through 19, are about "Getting it right." I've subtitled that section, "On getting married and not getting happier or healthier or more connected and not getting to live longer: What the research really does show and why."

Part III, chapters 20 through 36, are about "Getting it wrong." The short chapters are critiques of dubious claims about getting married and getting happier and healthier.

Finally, in **Part IV**, chapters 37 through 41, I take a step back to try to account for all the misinformation about marriage and single life. I also offer some suggestions for getting it right in the future.

If you read every chapter of this book, you will find that some of my arguments appear in multiple chapters. It would have been so great if I could have made those arguments just once, and thereby changed our understanding of what the research on marriage and single life really does show. I hope to keep trying for as long as it takes.

The chapters that first appeared as blog posts included many links. I have kept those links in both the e-book and paperback editions of this book. In the e-book, they are live; in the paperback, they let readers know what is available.

Sadly, misleading claims about the supposed benefits of marrying just keep coming, and will likely continue long after this book is published. But I won't stop reading the original research reports and offering my critiques. As they become available, I will add them to the collection at my website, "Everything you know about the benefits of marrying is wrong: The evidence." Enjoy!

Bella DePaulo
Summerland, CA
February 2015
BellaDePaulo.com

PART I

WHY YOU SHOULD ALWAYS BE SKEPTICAL OF CLAIMS THAT GETTING MARRIED MAKES YOU HAPPIER OR HEALTHIER OR BETTER OFF IN ANY OTHER WAY*

*Except for getting wealthier. Once you marry, you get more than 1,000 legal benefits and protections unavailable to single people – and that's just at the federal level

1

LIVING SINGLE:

LIGHTENING UP THOSE DARK, DOPEY MYTHS

[This chapter by Bella DePaulo first appeared in William R. Cupach and Brian H. Spitzberg (Eds.), *The Dark Side of Personal Relationships II* (pp. 409-439). New York: Routledge, 2011.]

When I was invited to write this chapter on living single for this new *Dark Side* volume, I was both honored and offended. Honored, because the *Dark Side* series is terrific. What self-respecting relationships scholar does not have a few volumes adorning a bookshelf? Offended, because how dare anyone suggest that the topic of living single belongs with other writings on ominous relationship topics such as rejection, narcissism, in-laws, aggression, and interpersonal violence?

I went back and forth with the editors, and they assured me that they did not mean to disparage singles. When they also quickly agreed to allow me to craft my own snarky subtitle, "Lightening up those dark, dopey myths," I agreed, too.

As I write this chapter, I am 55 years old and I have always been single. I have an inkling of what others think of people like me – people who are single long past the age at which most who will marry have already done so, some of them over and over again. Of course, I have my personal stories – at first, that's all I had – but now I have a whole passel of studies as well. Experimental research shows that perceptions others have of singles are rather dark. Compared to people who are married, singles are seen as sad, lonely, and self-centered. In the popular view of things, we singles are "alone" and "don't have anyone;" there's probably something wrong somewhere (DePaulo, 2006).

It is not just the aging singles who are seen that way, although older is linked with darker when it comes to perceptions of singlehood. Even 20-something year olds are perceived more negatively when they are single than when they are married, or when they are not in a romantic relationship, compared to when they are. More on all of that later.

Personally, I never had wedding fantasies. I never designed some big white dress in my head nor did I keep a mental list of bridesmaid candidates. Except for all of the singlism (the term I coined for the

1

stereotypes, stigma, and discrimination against singles), I've always liked living single. I rarely said so quite so explicitly, and anyway, I thought I was the exception. I had seen the many headlines proclaiming that if only I would get married, I would be happier, healthier, live longer, and all the rest. Many of the stories in the popular press were supposedly based on scientific research. For decades, most of my research was on another topic (the social psychology of deception), so I had not read any of the original journal articles myself. The party line about the transformative power of getting married did not seem to be challenged, so I believed it.

When I first decided to study single life rather than just practice it, I already had a storyline in mind. Singles did not enjoy the same levels of well-being as people who had gotten married, I thought, because they were targets of stereotyping and stigma, and were often socially excluded in a society so preoccupied with couples. I planned to look very closely at the literature on life outcomes, to see whether there were some subcategories of singles who were less disadvantaged (relative to people who got married) than others. That way, maybe I could start to figure out what it was about single life, other than singlism and matrimania (my term, again, for the over-the-top hyping of marriage and weddings), that accounted for singles' poorer outcomes.

Once I studied the literature and did some of my own research, I found that there were, indeed, negative perceptions of singles and evidence of discrimination as well. What I never did find, though, was any compelling evidence that getting married resulted in lasting improvements in happiness, health, or any other measure of well-being. That really surprised me. Eventually, I also figured out why the conventional wisdom about the supposed benefits of getting married was so wrong, and why even smart and serious scholars were getting it wrong.

My trip through the stacks of research on marital status left me with a whole different question. Rather than trying to explain why getting married resulted in psychological benefits, I needed to figure out why single people were faring much better than the conventional wisdom suggested. Plus, how could they be doing so well when they really were targets of singlism?

Before I tell you the rest of that story, though, let me first cover some of the basics. What do I mean by single? And, how unusual is it to be single in contemporary American society and around the globe?

Who Counts as Single?

The most straightforward definition of single is the *legal* one – single people are adults who are not officially, legally married. The legal definition is consequential. It is the criterion for access to a wide variety of benefits and protections – more than 1,000 in federal statutes alone (DePaulo, 2006).

In everyday life, though, often what matters more is whether people are *socially* coupled or socially single. Here, the criteria are not so straightforward. Other people try to infer your coupled status from a variety of cues; for example, do you seem to be in a romantic relationship? Does it seem to be a long-term one? Are you living with the person? Whether you are considered socially coupled, though, does not depend on your sexual orientation; there are no culture wars over whether same-sex people can be coupled.

Individuals have their own perceptions of whether or not they are coupled. These *personal* definitions of coupled status may or may not correspond with other people's perceptions (the social definition).

Singles in Society: What is the Demographic Picture?

In 2007, the *New York Times* made a splash with the headline, "51% of Women Are Now Living Without Spouse" (Roberts, 2007). That number was calculated in ways I do not favor; for example, people 15 and older were included in the counts, thereby inflating the number of singles. I like to count starting at age 18.

As of 2007, according to the U.S. Census Bureau, 92.8 million Americans (18 and older, women and men) were legally single. That's 41.7% of the adult population. The legally single category includes people who are divorced, widowed, and have always been single. (The Census Bureau uses the label "never married" rather than always-single.) Cohabitors – now described by the Census Bureau as members of "unmarried-partner households" – are also included in those numbers. In 2006, there were 12 million cohabitors, including 1.56 million in same-sex households.

When the 12 million cohabitors are subtracted from the number of legally single people (and those who are separated continue to be left out of the count), there are 80.8 million Americans who are single. That's 36% of the adult population. Among those millions, in 2006, were 12.9 million single parents; 10.4 million were single mothers.

Perhaps the more remarkable statistic is that Americans now spend more years of their adult lives unmarried than married (DePaulo, 2006). This reversal of past patterns is the result of a number of converging demographic trends, including an increase in the age at which people first marry (if they marry), and a rate of divorce that continues to be high (if not still climbing). There are also many single women later in life; life-spans have been increasing, and women continue to outlive men.

The trend toward spending more time single is not specific to the United States. Across 192 countries, people who, by age 30, had always been single increased from 15% in the 1970s to 24% in the 1990s. The increase was greater for developed countries: In the 1990s, 38% of the women and 57% of the men reached the end of their 20s without ever marrying (World Fertility Report, 2003).

The growing number of singles in America, and the many years that American adults spend living single, is also noteworthy because the rate of marrying is so high. As Cherlin (2009) has documented in his research on Western nations, "The percentage of people who are projected to marry [in the United States] – close to 90 percent – is higher than elsewhere. Yet the United States has the highest divorce rate in the Western world, higher even than vanguard countries such as Sweden (p. 4)." Americans, says Cherlin, are on a "marriage-go-round," stepping on and off the marital ride more often than any other Westerners.

Are Single People Alone, Unattached, and Pining for a Partner?

In everyday life, people who are single are often described as "alone" or "unattached." This colloquial way of thinking seems to rest on the premise that unless you have a romantic partner, you don't have anyone – you are alone and unattached. Let's set aside the prejudice that only conjugal partners count, and look at the science. Do singles have important people in their lives or are they truly alone? If they do have people who are important to them, are their relationships with those people true attachments in the scientific sense? And if singles do have important people in their lives, and if they have true attachments too, aren't they still pining for romantic partners?

Personal Relationships of People Who Are Single

There have been hints, for as long as journalists and scholars have been conducting qualitative studies of single life, that single women are hardly alone. (Unfortunately, a disproportionate chunk of the research on singles is only about single women.) For example, an intensive study of 50 women, ages 65 to 105, who had always been single (Simon, 1987) showed that only one was socially isolated. The other 49 women had a total of 47 friends they were in touch with every day (16 of those friendships had been ongoing for more than 40 years), and another 98 friends with whom they were in contact once or twice a week. A more recent random sample survey of 1,714 American women, ages 25 to 72, showed that the women who had always been single and those who were previously married spent significantly more time with friends than did the women who were currently married (Carr, 2008).

Analyses of two more national surveys of Americans (including both men and women) revealed that people who have always been single do more to maintain interpersonal ties than currently married people do (with the previously married typically in between). Specifically, always-single adults are more likely to visit, contact, advise, and support their siblings, and they are also more likely to socialize with, encourage, and help their friends and neighbors (Gerstel & Sarkisian, 2006). Adults who have always been single are also more likely to be the keepers of intergenerational ties. They more often stay in contact with their parents and give or receive practical, emotional, or financial help. Differences in time demands, resources or needs, or extended family characteristics do not account for these disparities. When all of those factors, as well as demographic ones, are controlled, single people still do more to maintain relationships with their parents than currently married people do (Sarkisian & Gerstel, 2008).

Even in later life, single cannot be equated with "alone." A prospective study of 1,532 Americans, 65 and older, who started out married, showed that those who became widowed did not become more isolated (Ha, 2008). Six months after becoming widowed, they had more support from their adult children than they had before. Eighteen months into their widowed life, they were less likely to have a confidant than they were when they were married and they were no longer receiving heightened support from their grown children. However, by then they were more likely to have support from friends and relatives.

Attachment Relationships of People Who Are Single

Research on adult attachments (like most other research on adult relationships) has focused overwhelmingly on people who are coupled. The first few studies of the attachments of single adults are beginning to appear, and they provide a stern note of caution to those who are tempted to continue describing single people as "unattached."

In a study of 812 Australians, ages 16 to 90, Doherty and Feeney (2004) asked about four vital attachment components. The participants could nominate up to five people in response to questions about having a *secure base* ("who do you feel will always be there for you if you need them?"), a *safe haven* ("who do you turn to for comfort when you are feeling upset or down?"), a target for their *proximity-seeking* ("who is it important for you to see/talk with regularly?") and a person whose absence creates *separation protest* ("who do you not like to be away from?").

The authors used a stringent criterion for what they called a "full-blown attachment." To qualify, the attachment figure had to be named as one of the most important on all four components. (It was possible to have more than one such attachment.) Of those people who did have romantic partners (whether married or not), 74% had full-blown attachments to their partner.

Is it possible to have a full-blown adult attachment relationship that is not with a romantic partner? Yes. Thirty-percent had full-blown attachments to at least one friend, 22% had such attachments to at least one sibling, 40% had a full-blown attachment to their mother, 16% to their father, and 40% who had offspring had a full-blown attachment to at least one of them.

The authors also calculated each person's primary attachment figure – the person with the highest score across all four components, regardless of whether that primary attachment was a full-blown one. For 77% of coupled people, their partner was their primary attachment figure. For the single (uncoupled) people, their primary attachment figure was most often a friend, 37%; their mother, 37%; an offspring, 11%; a sibling, 10%; or their father, 5%.

A second study compared the attachments of coupled people to singles who reported that they had not been in a committed relationship for at least three years and probably would not be within the next year or so (Schachner, Shaver, & Gillath, 2008). In addition to assessing the four components, the authors measured two dimensions, anxiety (e.g., "I worry about being abandoned"), and avoidance (e.g., "I feel comfortable depending on others," reverse-scored).

Overall, the singles and couples did not differ on anxiety or avoidance, nor were there any differences when the women were considered separately. Looking just at the men, there was a difference, but only for anxiety: The single men reported more attachment anxiety than the coupled men.

The singles and couples also did not differ in the number of people who fulfilled the four different attachment needs for them. Couples, of course, more often named partners as attachment figures than singles did. Singles were more likely than couples to name best friends as the people they especially liked to see and talk to regularly (proximity), and they were more likely to mention sisters as a secure base (a person with whom they felt secure, comfortable, and encouraged).

Are Single People Pining for a Partner?
Perhaps one of the most persistent beliefs about people who are single is that what they care about, more than anything else, is becoming unsingle (DePaulo, 2006). Research suggests that this conventional wisdom is a myth. The Pew Internet & American Life Project surveyed more than 3,000 American adults of all ages and marital statuses (Rainie & Malden, 2006). They asked the single

participants (divorced, widowed, and always-single) whether they were in a committed relationship and whether they were looking for a partner. Twenty-six percent said that they were already in a committed relationship. The biggest group, though, 55%, said that they were not in a committed relationship *and* that they were not looking for a partner. Only 16% said that they were not in a committed relationship but were looking. (The other 3% did not answer.) Even when the younger singles (ages 18 to 29) were analyzed separately, the number who said that they were not in a committed relationship but were looking increased to just 22%.

Later in life (65 and older), among the widowed, men are more likely than women to remarry. Yet, in her analysis of the data from the Changing Lives of Older Couples study, Carr (2004) found that 18 months after the death of their spouse, fewer than half of the men were interested in remarrying or even dating. What was important was whether they had better than average emotional support from friends; if so, they were no more interested than women were in dating or remarrying.

Implications of Getting Married: Cracking the Code of the Scientific Research

Now I want to turn to the heart of the matter. What does the social science research really say about the implications of getting married for health, happiness, or anything else that interests you? Before I get to the substance, stay with me while I describe my favorite hypothetical study. Understanding what's wrong with this study is key to figuring out what has gone so terribly wrong in the story that has been told about marital status in the popular press, and sometimes even in the scientific literature.

This make-believe study is about a make-believe drug I'll call Shamster. It is not a drug for people who are ailing, but instead for people who just want to feel better than they already do. The drug company that is peddling Shamster offers the drug to 2,200 people in 48 states. All of the people get to decide for themselves whether or not they want to take Shamster. If they do decide to try it, they can stop taking it if they don't like it. Some of the people start taking Shamster but eventually can't get any more for reasons beyond their control.

After a while, the drug company asks all the people to answer the question, "Taking all things together, how happy would you say you are these days?" They record their answers on a 4-point scale, where 1 means "not at all happy"; 2 indicates "not too happy"; 3 corresponds to "pretty happy"; and 4 is the most positive response, "very happy."

In reporting the results, the drug company separates the participants into four groups. One is the group of people who decided to take the drug and are still on it. The other three groups are not on the drug. One of those never did take the drug. Another took it, disliked it (sometimes intensely), and stopped taking it. The last were those who took it for a while but then could not access it anymore.

The company was absolutely delighted with the results. Here are the mean happiness ratings for the four groups:

3.3   Drug (chose to take the drug and still on it)
3.2   No drug (never did chose to take it)
2.9   No drug – intolerable (took the drug at first but disliked it and stopped)
2.9   No drug – withdrawn (took the drug at first but could no longer access it)

The company wants to publish their study in the prestigious *New England Journal of Medicine* (NEJM). They also want to run ads touting the greater well-being of people taking Shamster than people not taking it. From all the research they've done so far, they have a good idea of how tolerable Shamster is – of the many thousands of people who have tried it, about 43% dislike it and decide not to continue. Now they have started the next series of studies. They are trying to learn what exactly it is about Shamster that makes it such a great drug.

Would you, as editor of *NEJM*, accept the Shamster study for publication? Okay, stop laughing. Let me make the question less preposterous: Would you, as the instructor for an introductory research methods class, accept this design for a study from an undergraduate? I didn't think so. What about the general television-viewing public? Suppose they saw an ad describing this study and its results fairly. (This is still a hypothetical so I can pretend that ads are even-handed.) So, viewers learn that people who never took the drug have happiness levels of 3.2 (out of 4). People who take the drug have happiness levels of 3.3, as long as you don't count the 43% of the people who took the drug, hated it, and refused to continue taking it (and whose happiness levels average out to 2.9). Do you think they would be persuaded that they, too, should take the drug?

Getting Married and Getting Happy

The Shamster study is representative of much of the published research on marital status and life outcomes. Seriously. In fact, the design and results that I reported are from a real study (Gove & Shin, 1989), based in fact on 2,200 Americans from 48 states who answered precisely the question I described previously. As you probably anticipated, the four hypothetical drug groups correspond to four actual marital status groups:

> Drug (chose to take the drug and still on it) = **currently married**
>
> No drug (never did choose to take it) = **always single**
>
> No drug – intolerable (took the drug at first but disliked it and stopped) = **divorced**
>
> No drug – withdrawn (took the drug at first but could no longer access it) = **widowed**

Scientists who set out to study the implications of getting married face a formidable obstacle that does not stand in the way of drug researchers – they cannot randomly assign people to get married, stay single, or get divorced or widowed. They can, though, be clear and accurate about what their results really do mean.

Descriptively, it is accurate to say that people who are currently married are slightly happier than those who are not currently married. However, it is *not* scientifically justifiable to say that they are happier *because* they got married. The divorced and widowed people got married, too, but they are less happy than the people who had always been single. It is not even appropriate to conclude that you will be happier if you get married and stay married. That would assume that if the divorced people had stayed married, they too would have been happier than single people.

In the study described above (Gove & Shin, 1989), the authors were appropriately cautious about their findings. Others who have used their work as the basis for claims about marriage have not always been so careful. For example, Waite and Gallagher's (2000) often-cited book, *The Case for Marriage:*

Why Married People Are Happier, Healthier, and Better Off Financially, is filled with references to studies similar this one to make their bogus case.

Apart from the ethically-impossible method of randomly assigning people to marital statuses, the next best approach is the longitudinal study of lives over time. The most impressive longitudinal study of happiness is based on more than 30,000 Germans, 16 and older, who have been reporting on their happiness once a year for 19 years and counting. Lucas and his colleagues have tracked participants' happiness as they got married and stayed married (Lucas et al., 2003; Lucas & Clark, 2006), became widowed (Lucas et al., 2003) or divorced (Lucas, 2005; Lucas et al., 2003) or stayed single (reported in DePaulo, 2006). Life satisfaction was rated on an 11-point scale, 0 to 10, with higher numbers indicating greater happiness.

Those who got married and stayed married during the course of the study (comparable to the currently married group in cross-sectional research) became slightly happier around the time of the wedding (about one-quarter of a point), then they went back to being about as happy as they were when they were single. By getting married, they did not become lastingly happier – they just enjoyed a brief honeymoon effect. Those who got married and then divorced were already becoming less happy, rather than more so, as their wedding day drew nearer. Then their happiness continued to decrease until the year before their divorce became official.

At the start of the study, those who would stay single were slightly less happy (7.0) than those who would eventually marry and stay married (7.2), and slightly happier than those who would eventually marry and then divorce (6.9). The happiness of the single people declined about four-tenths of a point over the course of the study, reaching a low of 6.6. For most years of the study, the people who stayed single reported greater happiness than those who married and then divorced. Their happiness levels never reached the low point experienced by those who divorced (6.2) or became widowed (6.0).

Note, too, that the midpoint of the happiness rating scale was 5. The mean for the single people was always squarely on the happy end of the scale – especially for those who stayed single the entire time.

Getting Married and Getting Healthy

Now let's examine the related claim that people who marry become healthier. The key studies are again longitudinal, but I'll start with the more commonplace cross-sectional reports.

Starting in 1972, a nationally representative sample of Americans, ages 25 to 80, has been recruited each year to describe their health as part of the National Health Interview Survey. (They are different people each time.) In 2008, Liu and Umberson reported the results of the first 31 years of surveys. Participants were asked to rate their health as poor, fair, good, or excellent. Here are the percentages of people who rated their health as either good or excellent for 2003, the most recent data available to the authors:

% with good or excellent health	Marital status
92.9	Currently married
92.6	Always single
91.0	Divorced
89.4	Separated
86.6	Widowed

The pattern is similar to what we saw for happiness. Those who stayed single are barely distinguishable from those who got married and stayed married. Those who got married then separated, divorced, or became widowed have lower levels of overall health than those who stayed single or stayed married, but the differences are not big. Comparable patterns for American samples have been reported by Marks et al. (2004) and by the CDC (2004, and critiqued in DePaulo, 2006). In a brief review of the health and marital status literature, Rook and Zettel (2005) also described similar findings.

One cross-sectional study is especially worth noting because it included measures of 18 different health conditions, including fatal chronic diseases as well as less serious problems. Pienta, Hayward, and Jenkins (2000) analyzed the first wave of data from the Health and Retirement Study, collected in 1992 from a nationally representative sample of 9,333 Americans between the ages of 51 and 61. The adults who had always been single more closely approximated the currently married in their health than did the divorced or widowed. In fact, for six of the 18 measures – including four of the six fatal chronic illnesses – the always-single adults had nonsignificantly better health than the currently married. They also had better health than the divorced and widowed on all 18 measures. (Significance tests were not reported for those comparisons.)

In a sample of 11,131 Canadians (White, 1992), adults who had always been single reported health that was as good or better than that of adults who were currently married. As shown below, their reports of their overall health (1 = poor; 4 = excellent) were the same. More of the singles, though, reported having no health problems, and they also reported fewer doctor visits than did any other group. Again, those who got married and then got unmarried had somewhat worse health.

Marital Status	% with no problems	# doctor consultations	subjective health
Curr. married	51	2.4	**3.1**
Always single	**68**	**2.2**	**3.1**
Divorced	50	2.5	3.0
Widowed	20	2.7	2.7

A study of more than 10,000 Australian women is also telling. Cwikel, Gramotnev, and Lee (2006) wondered how women's health held up by the time they reached their mid-70s. They compared women who had always been single and had no children to married women who had no children and those who did have children, and to previously married women with and without children. The always-single women did the same or better than the other 70-something year-old women on every measure. They were the least likely to have had a diagnosis of a major health problem, least likely to be smokers and most likely to be non-drinkers. They were the most physically active and had the best body mass index. The always-single women did not differ from the other women in number of symptoms, doctor visits, falls requiring medical attention, hospital admissions, surgical procedures, or their overall levels of physical functioning. They were also no more likely to be receiving care from a family member.

As with happiness (or any other outcome), the most compelling conclusions come from studies in which the same people are followed over time. With regard to health, there are no longitudinal datasets comparable to the one on happiness that Lucas and his colleagues have been analyzing, with decades of data on the same people. There are, however, some shorter-term longitudinal studies of the health implications of staying single, getting married, or getting unmarried (divorced or widowed).

When cross-sectional data show that the currently-married report better health than the previously married (and sometimes, the always-single), is that because it is good for your health to get married (the transition from being single to being married) or because it is bad for your health when a marriage ends? Williams and Umberson (2004) addressed this question with a nationally representative sample of Americans, ages 24 to 98, who were asked to rate their health at two different points in time, separated by about four years. Their conclusion was that "marital status differences in health appear to reflect the strains of marital dissolution more than they reflect any benefits of marriage" (p. 81). The only evidence that getting married was good for health was for men, and only for the year or so just after the wedding (comparable to the honeymoon effect that Lucas found for happiness). For men, becoming widowed was a hazard to their health, but only initially. Getting divorced was actually good for men's health when it happened during young adulthood or mid-life. Women got no health bonus for marrying, not even during the honeymoon period. The fate of their health over the course of the four years did not depend on whether they stayed single, got married, or got unmarried.

Another longitudinal study of health began in 1992 with more than 9,000 Americans between the ages of 51 and 61 (Dupre & Meadows, 2007). They were interviewed every other year until 2000. The rates of disease for the people who had always been single were compared to a select set of married people – those who got married and stayed married. There were no differences. (Don't look for that in the abstract or text – the authors don't mention it. You can only find it in Tables 2 and 3.) There was only one finding suggesting that getting married had implications for health, and it was a negative one: Women who got married at age 18 or younger were at greater risk of developing a serious health problem. The authors concluded that what matters more than your current marital status is whether you have gotten married and unmarried repeatedly (usually a bad thing), and how long you have been in each marital status (longer is typically better for health, although there are exceptions).

In one last longitudinal study, a nationally representative sample of 9,775 Canadians, ages 20 to 64, was assessed in 1994 or 1995 and again two years later (Wu & Hart, 2002). The authors were particularly interested in marital transitions, and they also wanted to see whether the health implications of cohabitation would differ from those for marriage. The very first sentence of their article proclaimed that "Empirical research has almost unequivocally found that the married enjoy better mental and physical health than the unmarried (p. 420)." If you have read nothing about marital status and outcomes other than this chapter, you already know that there are problems with this statement and risks to using it as grounds for predicting that getting married would result in better health. The authors, though, were undeterred. Not only did they think that getting married would improve health; they also predicted that "the transition from singleness to a nonmarital union will bring about positive health outcomes (p. 422)," too.

Wrong! Transitioning from single status into either a cohabiting relationship or into marriage just did not matter with regard to health, either for men or for women. It didn't matter for overall self-reported health and it didn't matter for "functional health," an index comprised of vision, hearing, speech, pain, discomfort, mobility, dexterity, cognition, and emotion. (Relevant to the next section of this chapter, it also didn't matter for a composite measure of depression.)

What did matter was becoming uncoupled (from either a marriage or a cohabiting relationship). For both the men and the women, dissolving a union resulted in worse physical health, greater depression, or both.

There was one more result that did not fit with the authors' opening declaration of the supposedly unequivocal health advantages of married people. Some of the people in the study stayed in their marital or cohabiting unions over the two-year period, and others stayed single. Guess whose health got worse during that time? The coupled people's! The authors can only speculate as to why that happened. My "favorite" suggestion of theirs is this one: "It is also possible that because only 2 years separate Time 1 and Time 2, some union conflicts have yet to lead to union dissolution. In such cases, a decline in physical or mental health may precede exiting a union (p. 430)." Get it? These troubled couples just haven't put an end to their marriage or union yet. Once they do, then they will be out of the "currently married" group, and the health of the people remaining in that group will look better. (Of course, none of the proposed interpretations took on the question of why the people who stayed single maintain their good health or even improved it.)

The last word goes to Liu and Umberson (2008). In the concluding paragraph of the report of their 31-year study (not longitudinal), they advise that "encouraging marriage in order to promote health may be misguided. In fact, getting married increases one's risk for eventual marital dissolution, and marital dissolution seems to be worse for self-rated health now than at any point in the past three decades" (p. 252).

Getting Married and Getting Depressed

In 2007, the website of MSNBC ran a story under the headline, "New treatment for depression – marriage." Before you head to the altar to cure your depression, let's see what the data really do say.

Cross-sectional research reveals a familiar pattern. For example, in a study of 1,338 Canadians ages 18 through 55 (Turner & Lloyd, 1999), the currently married and the always-single were indistinguishable in depressive symptomatology and in recent major depressive episodes, once the usual demographic factors are controlled. Even with controls, the previously married (divorced, in this study) still showed somewhat more depressive symptoms than the currently married and always-single. Marks (1996) reported similar findings for an American sample.

As always, longitudinal evidence is more persuasive, and there are a number of such studies of marital status and depression. A study of young adults found that those who got married between the ages of 21 and 24 did not become any less depressed than those who stayed single (Horwitz & White, 1991). A 7-year study of adults who were 18, 21, or 24 years old at the outset compared those who stayed single to the usual subset of those who got married – that is, only those who got married and stayed married (Horwitz, White, & Howell-White, 1996). The authors explained that they excluded anyone who got separated or divorced during the study "because they clearly are not deriving any benefits from marriage" (p. 899). You read that correctly. In a study of whether marriage is beneficial, the authors set aside those who clearly were not benefiting from marriage. Still, only the men, and not the women, became less depressed after marrying.

One particular longitudinal dataset, the National Survey of Families and Households (NSFH), has been analyzed repeatedly for clues to the links between marital status and depression (Frech & Williams, 2007; Lamb, Lee, & DeMaris, 2003; Marks & Lambert, 1998; Simon, 2002). In the study, a national sample of Americans 19 and older participated in 1987 or 1988 and again about five years later. Different investigators looked at different age groups and zeroed in on different comparisons. What had become customary was the practice of setting aside those who married and then split up when testing the hypothesis that getting married results in less depression.

The most recent analysis of the NSFH, and one that included more potentially relevant factors than the others, was reported by Frech and Williams (2007). They thought that any depression-relevant implications of getting married might depend on whether people were depressed before they married. They compared the people who were single at the first assessment and who stayed single to those who married and stayed married. Anyone who got married and then divorced was removed from the analysis. The 20% of the people who started out depressed at the first point in time did become less depressed if they married. The other 80%, who were not depressed at the outset, did not feel significantly less depressed upon marrying than did the people who stayed single. The authors added one more qualification: "In most cases, above-average marital happiness was necessary for conferring the psychological benefits of a transition into marriage." So, in conclusion, people who get married become less depressed than people who stay single, as long as (a) you focus on the 20% of the people who were already depressed before they married; (b) you set aside anyone who got married and then divorced; (c) you look primarily at those who, once they married, experienced greater than average marital happiness; and (d) your married group has been married no more than five years. By the way, this is the study that was the basis of MSNBC's claim that marriage is a new treatment for depression.

Getting Married and Getting Less Lonely

In review papers (e.g., Cacioppo & Hawkley, 2005), it is easy to find claims that marriage is linked to lower levels of loneliness. Go to the original sources that are cited, though (e.g., de Jong-Gierveld, 1987; Tornstam, 1992), and interpretive problems become immediately apparent. The data are cross-sectional, and all of the unmarried people, including those who were previously married, are considered together, and compared to those who are currently married. So it is impossible to see the differences between those who actually did get married before becoming unmarried and those who stayed single.

Even studies in which the previously married are included with the always-single do not always show clear evidence that marriage is linked with less loneliness. Hawkley and her colleagues (2008), for example, found no overall difference between the currently married and the currently unmarried. A difference favoring the currently married was evident only when a subset of the currently married was compared to all of the unmarried – those who consider their spouse to be a confidant. In another example (Rokach, Matalon, Rokach, & Safarov, 2007), there were no differences in loneliness between the women who were currently married and all of the unmarried women; among the men, there was a significant difference favoring the currently married for only one of five loneliness subscales.

In a study of people 65 and older (Victor et al., 2005), those who had always been single, the currently married, and the previously married were all considered separately. The always-single people were lonelier than the currently married, but less lonely than the widowed. The divorced were similar to the always-single in their loneliness. As with other outcome variables, such as happiness and health, it is instructive to look at overall rates of the experience in question. Consistent with the story that is unfolding, rates of loneliness were generally low in all groups. For example, among the always-single people, only 9% said that they were often or always lonely, and 46% said they were never lonely.

Sometimes emotional loneliness – the absence of closeness or intimacy – is distinguished from social loneliness – the lack of a network of social ties. If marriage is a special site for intimacy, then it should be particularly protective against emotional loneliness. In a study of 55- to 89-year olds in which the currently married, the always-single, the divorced, and the widowed were all considered separately (Dykstra & de Jong Gierveld, 2004), there were bigger differences among the groups in emotional loneliness than social loneliness. For the men, emotional loneliness was most intense among the widowed and least among the currently married. Among the women, the previously married (widowed and divorced) were the most emotionally lonely. Women who had always been single reported very low levels of emotional loneliness, and were just as unlikely to be lonely as the women who were currently married. Remember, these were women averaging 72 years of age who had always been single. Stereotypically, they are the "old maids" living alone in their tiny apartments with a pack of cats. In fact, though, no other groups of women experience less emotional loneliness than they do.

There are some longitudinal studies of loneliness in which the currently married, previously married, and the always-single are all considered separately. However, they are studies of older adults, so it is not possible to discern the implications for loneliness of becoming married for the first time (Jylha, 2004; Wenger & Burholt, 2004). What the studies do suggest is that one of the greatest vulnerabilities to loneliness in later life is the transition into widowhood. Stability – which can come from remaining married or remaining unmarried – can protect against loneliness.

Getting Married and Getting Sex

There is no longitudinal study about sex, comparable to the Lucas studies of happiness, in which the same people are followed over time, as they enter, exit, or remain in various marital statuses, and report on the frequency and quality of their sexual experiences along the way. All we have, then, are cross-sectional data.

Perhaps the most comprehensive contemporary study of sexual behavior is the National Sex Survey, conducted by Laumann and his colleagues (Laumann, Gagnon, Michael, & Michaels, 1994). They compared the currently married with the previously married (divorced, separated, or widowed) and with those who had always been single. For the previously married and the always-single, they looked separately at those who were cohabiting and those who were not.

Table 1: National Sex Survey: Frequency of Sex and Emotional Satisfaction

	Frequency of Sex: More Than Once a Week (%)		Extremely Emotionally Satisfied with Sex (%)	
	Men	Women	Men	Women
Currently married	43.4	38.5	48.9	42.1
Always single, cohabiting	55.9	59.8	35.2	44.1
Always single, not cohabiting	26.4	20.3	32.4	31.4
Divorced, separated, widowed, cohabiting	55.5	50.9	52.6	36.5
Divorced, separated, widowed, not cohabiting	25.0	20.5	23.0	27.4

NOTE: Based on Laumann et al. (1994), Tables 3.4 and 3.7. N for frequency of sex: 3,159. N for emotional satisfaction: 2,988.

Table 1 shows the percentages in each category who were having sex more than once a week and who were extremely emotionally satisfied with their sex. It is not the currently married people, but the cohabitors, who are having sex most frequently. Consistent with the usual trends, within the cohabitors, it is the always-single who score higher than the previously married. Even among those who are not married and not cohabiting, more than 20% are having sex more than once a week.

The story is similar for the percentage of people who are extremely emotionally satisfied with their sex. The most satisfied are the cohabitors – for men, the previously married cohabitors, and for women, the always-single cohabitors. The currently married are the next most satisfied. The group reporting the smallest percentage of people who were extremely emotionally satisfied with their sex, the previously married men who were not cohabiting, still had 23% who chose the most positive response option on a 5-point scale.

Canadians cannot save the hypothesis that marriage is linked to sexual bliss. A national sample of 1,582 Canadians (women only) responded to questions about three sexual concerns: experiencing a lower sexual desire than they would like, experiencing orgasms infrequently during intercourse, and having pain during intercourse (Gruszecki, Forchuk, & Fisher, 2005). The three marital status groups – currently married, divorced or separated, and always-single – did not differ in their experiences of pain or orgasms during intercourse. There was a significant difference in desire – it was lowest for the currently married.

Getting Married and Living Longer

This is a book about the dark side of relationships, and there is nothing darker than death. In popular accounts and even in some supposedly scientific reviews, getting married is said to be such a powerful transformation that it keeps death at bay. Or, as an esteemed scholar put it to me at dinner the other night, "Don't married people live longer?"

I can understand why people think this. Suppose you are just casually interested in the link between getting married and living longer. You're a scientist, so you look at the actual journal articles (and not just the headlines in the media), but this isn't your main area of interest or expertise, so you just read the abstracts. In one particularly good study of marital status and longevity – it was based on a representative national sample and it was a longitudinal study – the abstract ends with this: "**CONCLUSIONS**: Each of the non-marital status categories show elevated RR [relative risk] of death compared to married persons (p. 1047)."

Now let me tell you what you will discover if you read beyond the abstract. First, here are more of the details about the methodology. The National Longitudinal Mortality Study (NLMS) was the source of data from 281,460 Americans who were at least 45 years old when they were first assessed for this report (Johnson, Backlund, Sorlie, and Loveless, 2000). Their mortality was tracked for a maximum of 11 years.

The authors analyze mortality rates separately by eight different groups: men and women who are Black or White and when first assessed, were either 45 to 64 years old, or 65 and older. Within those eight groups, the authors compare mortality rates of three different unmarried categories – widowed, divorced, and always-single – to the mortality rates of the currently married. Once again, these are not comparisons of all of the people who ever got married to all of the people who stayed single; they are comparisons of the currently married to the various categories of currently unmarried.

Let's look first at the people who had always been single. Among the Blacks, there are four subgroups. In three of them, there is no difference in mortality risk between the currently married Blacks and the Blacks who had always been single. Only for the younger Black males was the mortality risk higher (and even for them, the risk was nonsignificantly lower than it was for the previously married). The always-single Whites did have higher mortality rates than their currently-married counterparts, though the effect was smaller for the older groups.

These findings alone undermine the claim in the abstract. The authors can only declare that "each of the non-married categories show elevated RR of death, compared to the married persons" if they pretend that they did not really include in their study any older Black men or any Black women of any age.

Now let's turn to the results for the currently divorced. In seven of the eight groups, the divorced people had higher mortality risks than the currently married. (The older Black men were the exception.) The mortality risks were generally similar for the widowed as for the always-single. As with other outcome variables, then, the risk is not so much in staying single as in getting married and then getting divorced.

So what does this study offer as an answer to the question posed by my dinner companion: Will you in fact live longer if you get married? Not if you are among the 43% or so who marry and then divorce. Unless you are a Black man and you've already made it to age 65, getting divorced probably means that you will have a shorter life. What if you got married, wanted to divorce, but forced yourself to stay married in hopes of living longer? There's no definitive, empirical answer to that. Theoretically, it is possible that staying in a marriage that is making you miserable could shorten your life rather than extending it.

If you marry and become widowed, your mortality risk will sometimes be higher, but not as consistently so as if you marry and then divorce. If you marry and never get divorced and never become widowed – well, that means you died before your spouse did.

The National Longitudinal Mortality Study tracked people for 11 years at most. There is another study (Tucker, Friedman, Wingard, & Schwartz, 1996), rarely if ever mentioned by those who tout the claim that getting married means getting to live longer. The participants were from the Terman Life-Cycle Study, and were less diverse than those in the NLMS. (They were almost all White, and only those who were above average in IQ were selected). Still, the study is significant because it is probably the longest-running study of mortality ever conducted. It started in 1921, with 1,528 eleven-year olds. Scientists followed the participants for as long as they lived. The people who lived the longest were those who stayed single and those who got married and stayed married. People who divorced, or who divorced and remarried, had shorter lives. What mattered was consistency, not marriage. The results were the same for the women and the men.

So What is the Dark Side of Living Single?

I will review four darks sides to living single: negative stereotypes, discrimination, interpersonal exclusion, and the experiences of atypical singles who really are unhappily single.

Stereotypes of Singles

When my colleagues and I asked nearly 1,000 college students to think about either single or married people and list the characteristics that came to mind, we received an outpouring of glorification of married people and derogation of singles (Morris, DePaulo, Hertel, & Ritter, in press). For example, 32% of those who were asked to describe married people spontaneously noted that they were loving; not one person described singles that way. Of those assigned to describe married people, 49% said they were kind, caring, and giving; only 2% of the participants describing singles listed those attributes. By less dramatic margins, married people were also more often described as happy, secure, faithful, and compromising. Singles were more likely to be described as lonely and shy. There were just two ways that singles were perceived more positively: They were more often characterized as independent, and as sociable, friendly, or fun.

We also did studies in which we created profiles of single and married people that were identical except for their marital status and other experimentally manipulated characteristics (DePaulo & Morris, 2006; Morris et al., in press). For example, in some studies, half of the people were described as 25 years old, and the others as 40. We showed the profiles to groups of undergraduates and people from the community and asked them to rate them on various scales. All of the groups rated the singles as less well-adjusted, more socially immature, more self-centered, and more envious than the married people (though also more independent and career-oriented). The differences were especially striking when participants were rating the 40-year olds, but they also saw the 25-year old single people more negatively than the 25-year old married people whose profiles were otherwise identical.

More than half of all Americans have not yet married by age 25, so it was sobering to find that even such young singles were stereotyped. In a subsequent study (Morris et al., in press), we created profiles of people who were all described as students, and manipulated whether they were currently single, currently coupled, previously coupled, or always single. Even using the standard of coupling rather than marriage, the young people in our profiles were regarded more negatively when they were not currently in a romantic relationship or when they had not previously been in one.

Discrimination Against Singles

Single people are treated less fairly than married people in many ways, including some that are sanctioned by law (DePaulo, 2006; DePaulo & Morris, 2006). For example, employers can offer health benefits for spouses of married workers (and sometimes domestic partners), while not offering any comparable benefits to a sibling, a parent, a close friend or any other important person in the lives of people who are single. That's unequal compensation for the same work. Under the Family and Medical Leave Act, married people in eligible workplaces can take leave to care for a spouse, but single people cannot take advantage of the Act to care for anyone in their generation – nor can any of their peers take leave to care for them. The Social Security benefits earned by a married worker go to the spouse upon the worker's death; those earned by a single worker go back into the system.

Married men are paid more than single men, even when both are similar in age and work experience (reviewed in DePaulo, 2006). Whenever married couples pay less per person for auto insurance, club memberships, travel packages, or anything else, they are being subsidized by the single people who are paying more.

In an analysis of a nationally representative sample, Byrne and Carr (2005) found that single people report experiencing more discrimination in everyday life than married people do; for example, they receive poorer service in restaurants and experience more condescending attitudes in their interpersonal interactions.

There is also experimental evidence of housing discrimination against singles (Morris, Sinclair, & DePaulo, 2007). In three studies, participants read descriptions of three comparable applicants for a rental property and indicated the applicant to whom they would prefer to rent the property. Rental agents were far more likely to prefer a married couple (60%) to a cohabiting romantic couple (23%) or a pair of friends (17%). The undergraduates were even more biased; 80% of them chose the married couple, compared to 12% who chose the cohabiting couple and 8% who chose the friends. Undergraduates also greatly preferred a married couple (70%) to a single woman (18%) or a single man (12%). What's more, people don't think there is anything wrong with these biases. When participants in another study read about housing discrimination against singles, they reported that the practice was more fair and legitimate than similar housing discrimination against African Americans, gay people, or obese people (Morris et al., 2007).

Interpersonal Exclusion of Single People

As a romantic relationship becomes more serious, the couple spends more time alone (Milardo, Johnson, & Huston, 1983; Surra, 1985). Acquaintances and casual friends are marginalized gradually; close friends may still be included in some plans, but their opinions are taken less seriously (Johnson & Leslie, 1982). It cannot be determined from these studies whether the friends who are ditched as couples become closer are disproportionately single, but that does seem to be the perception of single people (DePaulo, 2006, 2009). Divorced and widowed people report something similar: married couples become less central to their lives than they were when they were still married themselves (Milardo, 1987; Morgan, Carter, & Neal, 1997). Again, it is not clear whether the newly single withdraw from married couples, whether they are excluded, or both.

Experiences of Atypical Single People

There is one more significant dark side to living single. I've reviewed the literature showing that most single people are doing just fine and are not pining for a partner. Still, there are more than 92 million unmarried Americans, and the typical description does not fit them all. If you are a single person who truly and deeply wants to be coupled, then all of the upbeat statistics in the world will not brighten your life.

Into the Future

We need to think more broadly and less stereotypically as we plan and evaluate research, and as we consider the real lives that single people lead. Here are some suggestions.

Reading or Reviewing Marital Status Research? Here Are Some Things to Keep in Mind

Imagine, fellow researchers, that you could take the 43% of the people in the key group in your study who are least compliant with your hypothesis, and just set them aside. Would your pet hypothesis look better if you tested it with the remaining 57% of the participants?

As of 2000, the likelihood of a marriage ending in divorce was at least 43% (Schoen & Canudas-Romo, 2006). When people doing marital status research remove from the group of people who got married all those who divorced, they are doing something comparable. If researchers want to make statements about the implications of getting married, then they need to include in the married group all those who ever got married, just as a drug company would have to base its effectiveness studies on all people who ever took the drug, and not just those who took it and liked it and kept taking it.

When investigators find that the currently married do better in some way or another and then ask what it is about getting married that is so beneficial, they neglect a key answer: The currently married look better not because they got married, but because those who got married, hated it, and got divorced were taken out of the got-married group – or even used as evidence for how great it is to get married (as when marriage is extolled on the grounds that the currently married look better than the previously married).

Amazingly, though, even with this tremendous advantage accorded to the currently married group, they do not always do better than people who have always been single. When they do have better outcomes than the always-single, often the differences are unimpressive. Looking at all marital status groups, when one does less well than the others, it is typically the people who got married then got divorced or became widowed. Even for them, the negative implications of transitioning out of marriage often diminish over time.

But isn't it okay to say, in a purely descriptive way, that people who are currently married sometimes have better outcomes than people who currently are not married? It is, in the same way that it is fine to say that people currently taking Shamster are sometimes better off than people who never took it or who took it and then stopped taking it because they hated it. You can say that, but you can't imply that if only you would get married, you too would have better outcomes. You could not even say that if you got married and stayed married, then you would have better outcomes, because that assumes that if divorced people had just stayed together, everything would be fine.

There are other ways in which the deck has been stacked in favor of the currently married in marital status research. Consider, for example, studies in which the currently married do *not* do better than other groups overall, and so researchers then focus on a subset of the currently married, such as those who are especially happy in their marriages or those who view their spouse as a confidant, to see if they look better than the singles. Do you see the problem? There is no comparable selection with regard to the singles. So, the happiest married people are not compared to the happiest single people; instead, the happiest married people are compared to all single people. It is comparable to a drug company claiming that people who take the weight-loss drug Blogus, and who also exercise, lose more weight than all the people who do not take Blogus, including those who do and do not exercise.

Doing Research? Here Are Some Suggestions

If I wanted to stay in my place and write the expected chapter on marital status research, I would make the predictable suggestions for future research. I might say, for instance, that when we compare single and married people, we need to attend more to the different varieties of singles, such as rich and poor singles, singles of different races and ethnicities, singles of different sexual orientations, and singles in different parts of the world. I'd also say that we need to learn more about how cohabitation is relevant to our questions about marital status, and how we may need to evaluate earlier studies of cohabitation – when the practice was less commonplace and more stigmatized – differently than more recent ones. I'd also underscore the importance of longitudinal research.

All of those are worthwhile directions for future research, but if that's all we did, then years from now, we'd still be kicking around in the same old box of conventional wisdom. The problem is that such suggestions do nothing to challenge the assumption that marital (or coupled) status, and that status alone, should be at the center of our quest to understand our interpersonal lives.

There's something wrong with that. Actually, several things. First, now that Americans are spending more years of their adult lives unmarried than married, it is misguided to focus so overwhelmingly on marriage. Second, if getting married really were essential to a happy or healthy life, people who have always been single could not be doing as well as they are. To explain how singles can do so well, despite all of the singlism and matrimania, takes a different perspective. Third, looking so intently at the marital relationship, to the neglect of other relationships and life interests and pursuits, does an injustice to married people, too.

An open-minded and broad-ranging approach to the study of adult relationships would not begin with the question of whether or not a person is married or coupled. Instead, a different set of questions would prevail. For example: Who are the important people in your lives? What do the concentric circles of your relationship life look like – who is in that innermost circle? Who are the people in the circles that emanate outward, including the circles of people who are not necessarily emotionally close but significant nonetheless (Fingerman, 2009)? What does your relationship portfolio look like, relative to what you wish it would look like? And, too, let's put the whole panoply of relationships into the context of the entirety of our lives. Are you developing not just your relationship portfolio but your life portfolio? Are you pursuing the interests and passions that motivate and define you? Do you have not just the time with other people that you would like to have, but also your ideal quotient of solitude?

Individual researchers who wish to focus on coupling should of course feel free to do so. But more of us need to break free of that conventional path, because the totality of our scholarship has fallen short of the big picture of our adult lives. In journals that publish adult relationship research, the studies that have appeared in their pages have overwhelmingly been examinations of marriage and coupling; forays into the wide-ranging world of friendship, for instance, or relationships with siblings, are harder to find (Fingerman & Hay, 2002). Developmental journals, of course, are stuffed with studies of friendship. It is as if the intellectual community as a whole has decided that friends are for kids.

Influenced, perhaps, by the Ideology of Marriage and Family (DePaulo & Morris, 2005a, b), in which it is assumed that just about everyone wants to marry, scholars look for evidence of misery and disease in the lives of people who are single, not stopping to ask first if living single is what they prefer (with rare exceptions, such as Dykstra, 1995). We are appropriately sensitive to the risks of feeling alone, so we have produced a cottage industry of studies of loneliness. Studies of solitude, on the other hand, are rare. This disproportion, too, seems to miss something significant about the way we are currently living our lives. There are now fewer American households comprised of married parents and their children than of people living solo. This is a stunning change from, say, 1970, when 40% of households were comprised of mom, dad, and the kids, and only 17% were one-person households (see DePaulo & Morris, 2005a, for more details). We need to take seriously the possibility that more people are living solo not because they are isolated and lonely, but because they value their own time and space, and that living alone does not always mean being alone.

We need to get beyond the focus on just the one most important person in our lives, even if that person is a friend rather than a conjugal partner. Looking at our personal communities, rather than just one significant other, tells us something about vulnerability and resilience. Spencer and Pahl (2006) made that clear in their research in which they asked adults to fill in the concentric circles of their own personal communities. Who, they asked, is there alongside you in that innermost circle? Who is in the other circles? The sets of circles corresponded to a variety of types of personal communities. Some, for instance, were partner-centered, typically with only the spouse in that most intimate circle. Not every married or coupled person had a partner-centered community; some of them had friends and family sprinkled throughout their inner circles. Other types of personal communities included friend-based and neighbor-based (in which friends and neighbors, respectively, have places in the inner circles) and professional-based communities, in which people put their professional helpers (such as therapists or social workers) in their inner circle and friends or family are missing or peripheral.

So which two personal communities were most likely to be linked to poorer mental health? Unsurprisingly, professional-based communities took up one of the slots. The other? Partner-based communities. As the authors noted, people whose personal communities are so dominated by a partner "lack diverse sources of support." They are vulnerable.

So Why Isn't Single Life the "Dark Side" of Our Lives?

Scholars and laypersons alike have screwed up the story of single life. We still think that singles are unhappy, unhealthy, and pining for a partner above all else when research shows that for most single people, that just isn't so. What happened?

Part of the problem, as Byrne and Carr (2005) have noted, is cultural lag. The place of singles in society has changed rapidly, and our perceptions have not caught up. In the late 1950s, before the advent of safe and effective birth control, before advances in reproductive science, and before the second women's movement brought greater opportunities for economic independence for women, marriage really was more central to adult life than it is now. Having sex and having children without stigma or shame were linked to marriage; for women, so too was financial security. Now, women can pick up the check at work and the sperm at the bank; children of single parents are equal to other children under the law; and many adults can buy their own table settings without the subsidies of a wedding shower. Marriage is a choice, not a requirement.

Our cultural conversations and media representations (DePaulo, 2006, 2009) and our academic journals and degree programs (DePaulo, Moran, & Trimberger, 2007) are mired in a marital state of mind. Take, for instance, the ways in which battles over same-sex marriage have dominated popular headlines and scholarly writings. In raising the question of why a person needs to have a partner of a different sex in order to have access to Family and Medical Leave, tax breaks, hospital visitation rights, and all the rest, few have taken a step back and asked why a person should need to have any kind of sexual partner at all in order to be protected and valued in such basic ways.

Our conventional wisdom, especially as laypersons, is rooted in the here and now, with too little cognizance of how different the profiles of interpersonal relationships, sexual norms, and life tasks have been at different times and in different places (e.g., Coontz, 2005; D'Emilio & Freedman, 1988; Gillis, 1996). When the Ideology of Marriage and Family is so dominant, even single people who like their single lives do not realize that there is nothing unusual about that. I didn't, until I read the research for myself. Maybe we are even reluctant to cop to our love of living single, as I once was. Maybe there are untold masses of single people keeping their happiness to themselves, thereby perpetuating the myth that we are all miserable and yearning to be coupled.

Another reason for our unenlightened take on single life is that the singlism that really does exist is either unacknowledged or deemed legitimate when it is recognized, as my colleagues and I showed in our studies of housing discrimination (Morris et al., 2007). Have you ever said to yourself, while reading this chapter, "Oh, she's biased because she is single?" It is something I've heard before. Yet, I have never, at conferences or classrooms or in casual conversations, heard anyone impugn the impartiality of scholars touting marital superiority, just because the scholars are married.

We need to make some cultural space for those who are single – and everyone else who resides outside of the traditional marriage and family mythology – to live their lives fully and unapologetically. As scholars, we cannot let cultural presumptions – for example, that getting married must be a good thing – mar the way we conduct and interpret our research. (The same applies to work on work on the outcomes of single parenting, which has also been plagued with interpretive problems [DePaulo, 2006, 2009].) Our research should not be biased in favor of single or married people, but should be based on the highest scientific standards.

Still Stuck on Romance? Here's the Singles-Friendly Payoff

I've been at this for a while, so I know that many readers of this chapter will remain unconvinced. Let me take a stab at one more argument – that tamping down singlism and matrimania is not just good for single people, it is also good for anyone who is, or who wants to be coupled.

Consider, for example, these snippets of research:

- In a prospective study (Gotlib, Lewinsohn, & Seeley, 1998), depression was assessed in a sample of 1709 high school students and their marital status was then tracked for years. The women who married young (before age 24) were more likely to have been depressed as adolescents than the women who were still single at that age. Once they did marry, their marriages were more likely to be troubled.
- In a longitudinal study, more than 8,000 adolescents were interviewed when they were between the ages of 12 and 17, and then again a year later (Joyner & Udry, 2000), those who became romantically involved between interviews experienced a greater increase in depression than those who did not. That happened even for the adolescents who were continuously involved, and not just for those who experienced break-ups.
- Or consider the research published under the title that says it all, "The strange case of sustained dedication to an unfulfilling relationship" (Slotter & Finkel, 2009). Why do people cling to a romantic partner who clearly is not fulfilling their needs?
- Why, too, do so many battered women return to their partners (Hamby, 1998)?

The explanations for these patterns are likely to be multi-faceted. Here I am simply making an observation. I think that the unchallenged dominance of the Ideology of Marriage and Family has made too many of us vulnerable. If we realize that single life can be a full and fulfilling life, then those who want to be coupled can pursue that goal from a position of strength – as something they want for all the positives they hope to get from it, and not just as something they end up in, or cling to, because they are so fearful of living single.

References

Byrne, A., & Carr, D. (2005). Caught in the cultural lag: The stigma of singlehood. *Psychological Inquiry*, *16*, 84-91.

Cacioppo, J. T., & Hawkley, L. C. (2005). People thinking about people: The vicious cycle of being a social outcast in one's own mind. In K. D. Williams, J. P. Forgas, & W. von Hippel (Eds.), *The social outcast: Ostracism, social exclusion, rejection, and bullying* (pp. 91-108). New York: Psychology Press.

Carr, D. (2004). The desire to date and remarry among older widows and widowers. *Journal of Marriage and Family*, *66*, 1051-1068.

Carr, D. (2008). Social and emotional well-being of single women in contemporary America. In R. M. Bell & V. Yans (Eds.), *Women on their own: Interdisciplinary perspectives on being single* (pp. 58-81). New Brunswick, NJ: Rutgers University Press.

Centers for Disease Control and Prevention. (2004). Marital status and health: United States, 1999-2002. Advance data, number 351. Hyattsville, MD: National Center for Health Statistics.

Cherlin, A. J. (2009). The marriage-go-round: The state of marriage and the family in America today. New York: Alfred A. Knopf.

Coontz, S. (2005). *Marriage, a history*. New York: Viking.

Cwikel, J., Gramotnev, H., & Lee, C. (2006). Never-married childless women in Australia: Health and social circumstances in older age. *Social Science & Medicine*, *62*, 1991-2001.

D'Emilio, J., & Freedman, E. B. (1988). *Intimate matters: A history of sexuality in America*. New York: Harper & Row.

de Jong-Gierveld, J. (1987). Developing and testing a model of loneliness. *Journal of Personality and Social Psychology, 53*, 119-128.

DePaulo, B. (2006). *Singled out: How singles are stereotyped, stigmatized, and ignored, and still live happily ever after.* New York: St. Martin's Press.

DePaulo, B. (2009). Single with attitude: Not your typical take on health and happiness, love and money, marriage and friendship. Seattle, WA: CreateSpace.

DePaulo, B., Moran, R. F., & Trimberger, E. K. (September 28, 2007). Make room for singles in teaching and research. *Chronicle of Higher Education, 54*, p. B44.

DePaulo, B. M., & Morris, W. L. (2005a). Singles in society and in science. *Psychological Inquiry, 16*, 57-83.

DePaulo, B. M., & Morris, W. L. (2005b). Should singles and the scholars who study them make their mark or stay in their place? *Psychological Inquiry, 16*, 142-149.

DePaulo, B. M., & Morris, W. L. (2006). The unrecognized stereotyping and discrimination against singles. *Current Directions in Psychological Science, 15*, 251-254.

Doherty, N. A., & Feeney, J. A. (2004). The composition of attachment networks throughout the adult years. *Personal Relationships, 11*, 469-488.

Dupre, M. E., & Meadows, S. O. (2007). Disaggregating the effects of marital trajectories on health. *Journal of Family Issues, 28*, 623-652.

Dykstra, P. A. (1995). Loneliness among the never and formerly married: The importance of supportive friendships and a desire for independence. *Journal of Gerontology: Social Sciences, 50B*, S321-329.

Dykstra, P. A., & de Jong Gierveld, J. (2004). Gender and marital-history differences in emotional and social loneliness among Dutch older adults. *Canadian Journal on Aging, 23*, 141-155.

Fingerman, K. L. (2009). Consequential strangers and peripheral ties: The importance of unimportant relationships. *Journal of Family Theory and Review, 1*, 69-86.

Fingerman, K. L., & Hay, E. L. (2002). Searching under the streetlight? Age biases in the personal and family relationships literature. *Personal Relationships, 9*, 415-433.

Frech, A., & Williams, K. (2007). Depression and the psychological benefits of entering marriage. *Journal of Health and Social Behavior, 48*, 149-163.

Gerstel, N., & Sarkisian, N. (2006). Marriage: The good, the bad, and the greedy. *Contexts, 5*, 16-21.

Gillis, J. R. (1996). *A world of their own: Myth, ritual, and the quest for family values*. New York: Basic Books.

Gotlib, I. H., Lewinsohn, P. M., & Seeley, J. R. (1998). Consequences of depression during adolescence: Marital status and marital functioning in early adulthood. *Journal of Abnormal Psychology, 107*, 686-690.

Gove, W. R., & Shin, H.-C. (1989). The psychological well-being of divorced and widowed men and women. *Journal of Family Issues, 10*, 122-144.

Gruszecki, L., Forchuk, C., & Fisher, W. A. (2005). Factors associated with common sexual concerns in women: New findings from the *Canadian Contraception Study. The Canadian Journal of Human Sexuality, 14,* 1-13.

Ha, J.-H. (2008). Changes in support from confidants, children, and friends following widowhood. *Journal of Marriage and Family, 70*, 306-318.

Hamby, S. L. (1998). Partner violence: Prevention and intervention. In J. L. Jasinski & L. M. Williams (Eds.), *Partner violence: A comprehensive review of 20 years of research* (pp. 210-258). Thousand Oaks, CA: Sage.

Hawkley, L. C., Hughes, M. E., Waite, L. J., Masi, C. M., Thisted, R. A., & Cacioppo, J. T. (2008) From social structural factors to perceptions of relationship quality and loneliness: The Chicago Health, Aging, and Social Relations Study. *Journal of Gerontology: Social Sciences, 63B*, S375-384.

Horwitz, A. V., White, H. R. (1991). Becoming married, depression, and alcohol problems among young adults. *Journal of Health and Social Behavior*, *32*, 221-237.

Horwitz, A. V., White, H. R., & Howell-White, S. (1996). Becoming married and mental health: A longitudinal study of a cohort of young adults. *Journal of Marriage and the Family*, *58*, 895-907.

Johnson, M. P., & Leslie, L. (1982). Couple involvement and network structure: A test of the dyadic withdrawal hypothesis. *Social Psychology Quarterly*, *45*, 34-43.

Johnson, N. J., Backlund, E., Sorlie, P. D., & Loveless, C. A. (2000). Marital status and mortality: The National Longitudinal Mortality Study. *Annals of Epidemiology, 10,* 224-238.

Joyner, K., & Udry, J. R. (2000). You don't bring me anything but down: Adolescent romance and depression. *Journal of Health and Social Behavior*, *41*, 369-391.

Jylha, M. (2004). Old age and loneliness: Cross-sectional and longitudinal analyses in the Tampere Longitudinal Study on Aging. *Canadian Journal on Aging*, *23*, 157-168.

Lamb, K. A., Lee, G. R., & DeMaris, A. (2003). Union formation and depression: Selection and relationship effects. *Journal of Marriage and Family*, *65*, 953-962.

Laumann, E. O., Gagnon, J. H., Michael, R. T., & Michaels, S. (1994). *The social organization of sexuality: Sexual practices in the United States*. Chicago: University of Chicago Press.

Liu, H., & Umberson, D. (2008). The times they are a changin': Marital status and health differentials from 1972 to 2003. *Journal of Health and Social Behavior*, *49*, 239-253.

Lucas, R. E. (2005). Time does not heal all wounds: A longitudinal study of reaction and adaptation to divorce. *Psychological Science*, *16*, 945-950.

Lucas, R. E., & Clark, A. (2006). Do people really adapt to marriage? *Journal of Happiness Studies*, *7*, 405-426.

Lucas, R. E., Clark, A., Georgellis, Y., & Diener, E. (2003). Reexamining adaptation and the set point model of happiness: Reactions to changes in marital status. *Journal of Personality and Social Psychology*, *84*, 527-539.

Marks, N. F. (1996). Flying solo at midlife: Gender, marital status, and psychological well-being. *Journal of Marriage and the Family*, *58*, 917-932.

Marks, N. F., Bumpass, L. L., & Jun, H. (2004). Family roles and well-being during the middle life course. In O. G. Brim, C. D. Ryff, & R. C. Kessler (Eds.), *How healthy are we? A national study of well-being at midlife* (pp. 514-549). Chicago: University of Chicago Press.

Marks, N. F., & Lambert, J. D. (1998). Marital status continuity and change among young and midlife adults: Longitudinal effects on psychological well-being. *Journal of Family Issues*, *19*, 652-686.

Milardo, R. M. (1987). Changes in social networks of women and men following divorce: A review. *Journal of Family Issues*, *8*, 78-96.

Milardo, R. M., Johnson, M. P., & Huston, T. L. (1983). Developing close relationships: Changing patterns of interaction between pair members and social networks. *Journal of Personality and Social Psychology*, *44*, 964-976.

Morgan, D., Carder, P., & Neal, M. (1997). Are some relationships more useful than others? The value of similar others in the networks of recent widows. *Journal of Social and Personal Relationships*, *14*, 745-759.

Morris, W. L., DePaulo, B. M., Hertel, J., & Taylor, L. C. (in press). Singlism -- another problem that has no name: Prejudice, stereotyping, and discrimination against singles. In T. G. Morrison & M. A. Morrison (Eds.), *The psychology of modern prejudice*. Hauppauge, NY: Nova Science Publishers.

Morris, W. L., Sinclair, S., & DePaulo, B. M. (2007). No shelter for singles: The perceived legitimacy of marital status discrimination. *Group Processes and Intergroup Relations*, *10*, 457-470.

Pienta, A. M., Hayward, M. D., & Jenkins, K. R. (2000). Health consequences of marriage for the retirement years. *Journal of Family Issues, 21*, 559-586.

Rainie, L., & Malden, M. (2006). Romance in America. Pew Internet and American Life Program. www.PewInternet.org http://pewresearch.org/pubs/1/not-looking-for-love, Retrieved September 4, 2009.

Roberts, S. (2007). 51% of Women Are Now Living Without Spouse. *The New York Times*, January 16. [I found the article online here, http://www.nytimes.com/2007/01/16/us/16census.html; it doesn't say where it appeared but the correction seems to imply it was on p. 1]

Rokach, A., Matalon, R., Rokach, B., & Safarov, A. (2007). The effects of gender and marital status on loneliness of the aged. *Social Behavior and Personality, 35*, 243-254.

Rook, K. S., & Zettel, L. A. (2005). The purported benefits of marriage viewed through the lens of physical health. *Psychological Inquiry, 16*, 116-121.

Sarkisian, N., & Gerstel, N. (2008). Till marriage do us part: Adult children's relationships with their parents. *Journal of Marriage and Family, 70*, 360-376.

Schachner, D. A., Shaver, P. R., & Gillath, O. (2008). Attachment style and long-term singlehood. *Personal Relationships, 15*, 479-491.

Schoen, R., & Canudas-Romo, V. (2006). Timing effects on divorce: 20th century experience in the United States. *Journal of Marriage and Family, 68*, 749-758.

Simon, B. L. (1987). *Never married women*. Philadelphia, PA: Temple University Press.

Simon, R. W. (2002). Revisiting the relationships among gender, marital status, and mental health. *American Journal of Sociology, 107*, 1065-1096.

Slotter, E. B., & Finkel, E. J. (2009). The strange case of sustained dedication to an unfulfilling relationship: Predicting commitment and breakup from attachment anxiety and need fulfillment within relationships. *Personality and Social Psychology Bulletin, 35*, 85-100.

Spencer, L., & Pahl, R. (2006). *Rethinking friendship: Hidden solidarities today*. Princeton, NJ: Princeton University Press.

Surra, C. A. (1985). Courtship types: Variations in interdependence between partners and social networks. *Journal of Personality and Social Psychology, 49*, 357-375.

Tornstam, L. (1992). Loneliness in marriage. *Journal of Social and Personal Relationships, 9*, 197-217.

Tucker, J. S., Friedman, H. S., Wingard, D. L., & Schwartz, J. E. (1996). Marital history at midlife as a predictor of longevity: Alternative explanations to the protective effect of marriage. Health Psychology, 15, 94-101.

Turner, J. R., & Lloyd, D. A. (1999). The stress process and the social distribution of depression. *Journal of Health and Social Behavior, 40*, 374-404.

Victor, C. R., Scambler, S. J., Bowling, A., & Bond, J. (2005). The prevalence of, and risk factors for, loneliness in later life: a survey of older people in Great Britain. *Ageing & Society, 25*, 357-375.

Waite, L. J., & Gallagher, M. (2000). *The case for marriage: Why married people are happier, healthier, and better off financially*. New York: Doubleday.

Wenger, G. C., & Burholt, V. (2004). Changes in levels of social isolation and loneliness among older people in a rural area: A twenty-year longitudinal study. *Canadian Journal on Aging, 23*, 115-127.

White, J. M. (1992). Marital status and well-being in Canada. *Journal of Family Issues, 13*, 390-409.

Williams, K., & Umberson, D. (2004). Marital status, marital transitions, and health: A Gendered life course perspective. *Journal of Health and Social Behavior, 45*, 81-98.

World Fertility Report (2003). Retrieved on October 31, 2008

http://www.un.org/esa/population/publications/worldfertility/World_Fertility_Report.htm

Wu, Z., & Hart, R. (2002). The effects of marital and nonmarital union transition on health. *Journal of Marriage and Family, 64*, 420-432.

2

NO STUDY HAS EVER SHOWN THAT GETTING MARRIED MAKES PEOPLE HAPPIER OR HEALTHIER –

AND NO STUDY EVER WILL

Summary

In the media and in academic writings, claims about the benefits of getting married are pervasive. People cannot be randomly assigned to get married or stay single or get divorced. Therefore, no study can ever support the causal claims that getting married makes people happier or healthier or better off in any other psychological or interpersonal way.

Most studies do not compare all people who have ever gotten married to those who stay single – the most appropriate comparison to make to answer the question of whether getting married results in better outcomes. Instead, only the currently married are compared to those not married. That approach greatly, and indefensibly, advantages the married group. Nonetheless, even with that built-in bias, results do not uniformly favor married people. Sometimes the always-single do best. When the married group appears to do best, often that edge is qualified by factors such as whether the adults are men or women, Black or White, younger or older, and whether the married people married recently or not so recently.

The typical social selection and social causation explanations for the purported advantages of the married group leave out significant alternatives, such as singlism. Theoretical analyses focus almost exclusively on the experiences of married people. Little has been said about the strengths of single people and the attractions of single life, leaving scholars mostly unprepared to explain the results of studies in which single people do as well as, or better than, married people.

Imagine that a pharmaceutical company has developed a new drug called Credulous and has conducted extensive testing. In all of their studies, participants get to choose whether to take the drug or not. Of those who do agree to take Credulous, close to half of them find their experiences so aversive that they refuse to continue taking the drug, even though they promised to continue for the entire length of the study.

In the research report that the drug company submits to the *New England Journal of Medicine* (NEJM), the authors set aside the people who refused to continue taking Credulous, and compare the people currently on the drug with those people not currently on the drug. They find that the people currently on the drug are doing better, and conclude that the drug is effective. In some of their analyses, the authors do not exclude the people who refused to continue taking the drug. Instead, they include those people with the people who never took the drug at all. So the analyses compare people who are currently taking the drug with everyone not currently taking the drug, including all those people who hated the drug (nearly half of those who ever tried it). They think this is entirely reasonable. If you want to know how well the drug is performing, they argue, don't you want to compare people who are currently on the drug to those who are not currently on it? So again, they find that the people currently taking Credulous are doing better than people not currently taking it, and they conclude that the drug made people better.

Would you recommend that the paper, and its conclusion about the effectiveness of Credulous, be accepted to the prestigious NEJM? Would you recommend that it be accepted to *any* journal? What if there had been a good reason to let people decide for themselves whether to take the drug or not; then would you accept the article? What if it had been submitted to you by an undergraduate taking an introductory research methods course – would you assign it a passing grade? Is there any circumstance under which you would allow researchers to set aside close to half of the people in the key condition, and compare them to everyone in the other condition(s)? This is such a violation of the most fundamental tenets of good scientific research that it seems silly even to pose the question in a serious academic journal.

The hapless pharmaceutical scientists get their paper rejected. They now understand that their cross-sectional research could never support their causal conclusions, so this time, they do something far more ambitious: They do longitudinal research. For reasons that are beyond the researchers' control, the people in their study still get to decide for themselves whether to take Credulous. The scientists start with people not on the drug, and follow them for years, assessing their health and well-being year after year. That way, they can see if outcomes change for the same people as they go from not taking the drug to taking it, and then continuing to take it. Using the same reasoning as before, they only include in their analyses the people who start taking Credulous and continue taking it over the entire course of the study. Again, they find that nearly half of the people who start taking the drug hate it and refuse to continue, and again, the scientists decide not to include them in their analyses. Now, if they find that people who take the drug feel better than they did before they started taking the drug, is it okay if they say that the drug is effective? Can they run advertisements saying that Credulous makes people feel better?

The longitudinal design is an improvement, but setting aside a substantial percentage of the people in the key group – even if it had not been nearly half – is still as indefensible, scientifically, as it was in the cross-sectional research. NEJM is unlikely to accept such a study. Teachers of undergraduates in their first research methods course might applaud their students' recognition of the superiority of a longitudinal design to a cross-sectional one, but they would still want them to understand why it is simply not acceptable, methodologically, to exclude all those people in the key group who *did* take the drug, just because they didn't like it and refused to continue to take it. You want them to realize how misleading it would be for the pharmaceutical company to advertise their drug as effective, based on studies in which the experiences of people who hated the drug are excluded. Maybe some instructors would even argue that the practice is unethical.

There should be no need to make any of these obvious points in a respectable scientific journal. When it comes to research on the implications of getting married for health and well-being, though, the need is pressing. The vast majority of studies on the topic are flawed in the fundamental ways I have described. Yet the results are used as the basis for claims that are as indefensible as the hypothetical ones made on behalf of the drug Credulous.

Researchers interested in the implications of getting married for health or well-being (or anything else) face an insurmountable methodological obstacle: It is impossible to randomly assign people to stay single or get married or get divorced or widowed. The gold standard of experimental research is out of reach. That's the main reason why no study has ever shown that getting married causes people to become happier or healthier – and no study ever will.

It is possible, though, to meet the most rigorous standards attainable within those constraints, and to be clear and accurate about the conclusions that are warranted on the basis of that research. As I will document later, bold claims about the benefits of marrying have appeared, unchallenged and often unqualified, in important legal documents, in popular publications with millions of readers, and in the lectures and writings of eminent social scientists. I will maintain that such claims are unwarranted.

My argument is not simply that it is impossible to do experimental research in which people are randomly assigned to marital statuses. I will also make the case that (1) too much of the research on marital status is not of the highest quality, even within the unavoidable restraints; (2) the prevailing designs indefensibly bias the results in favor of married people and against singles (as when people who get married and then get unmarried are excluded from the analyses); (3) even in studies in which marriage has been inappropriately advantaged, the results are not nearly as supportive of the purported benefits of marriage as many have claimed; and (4) interpretations of the results rarely acknowledge all of the serious limitations and alternative explanations. In fact, the explanations for the (presumed) marital advantage that so often appear in scholarly journals – selection and causation – routinely exclude some significant alternatives.

I will not offer an exhaustive review of outcome research on marital status; with probably thousands of relevant studies, that would be impossible. Instead, I will begin with what is perhaps the best available study of the implications of marrying (Musick & Bumpass, 2012): it is based on a nationally representative sample, it follows the same people over time, it assesses a variety of outcome variables (health, happiness, depression, self-esteem, and social ties), and analyses are reported in which everyone who married (and not just those who got married and stayed married) is included in the marriage group. Then I will consider a few illustrative studies of health and well-being. I looked for studies that are often cited in support of the supposed benefit of marrying and for studies that have certain strengths (e.g., they are longitudinal studies, or they are based on representative national samples). Studies of mortality are a special case because unlike, say, health or happiness, the ultimate outcome of death only happens once. It cannot be assessed each year as people get married or unmarried or stay single. That means that the kinds of studies that can be conducted, and the kinds of conclusions that can be drawn from those studies, are especially constrained. With those limits in mind,

I will look closely at a few illustrative studies to see if marriage is really as life-extending as has been claimed.

First, though, I will document the rise of single people. Then I will offer a brief sampling of claims that getting married makes people happier or healthier or better off in other ways, before proceeding to the heart of my critique. I end with a discussion of the claims that are and are not justified, and of the vast expanse of theoretical neglect when it comes to the study of the lives of people who stay single.

The Rise of Single People

There are beliefs about single and married people that are so widely accepted, and so rarely challenged, that DePaulo and Morris (2005) have described them as ideological. There are three marriage-relevant premises of their Ideology of Marriage and Family, defined by the assumptions that (1) "just about everyone wants to marry, and just about everyone does" (p. 57); (2) "a sexual partnership is the one truly important peer relationship" and (3) "those who have a sexual partnership are better people – more valuable, worthy, and important. Compared to people who do not have the peer relationship that counts, they are probably happier, less lonely, and more mature, and their lives are probably more meaningful and more complete" (p. 58)." In a series of studies of what they called "committed relationship ideology," Day and his colleagues (Day, Kay, Holmes, & Napier, 2011) documented the system justification motives contributing to the ideology.

In the U.S., the number of people who do marry at some point in their lives has been very high – probably about 90 percent (e.g., Goldstein & Kenney, 2001). Some try it over and over again. That pattern, though, seems to be changing. The number of Americans who are not married has been increasing for decades. By 2013, 105 million adults 18 and older (44 percent) were divorced or widowed or had always been single. The majority, 62 percent, were in the latter category. When people who are cohabiting are subtracted from the 105 million, that figure decreases only to 91 million (Census Bureau News, 2014). Americans now spend more years of their adult lives not married than married (DePaulo, 2006). A recent Pew Report (Wang & Parker, 2014) used Census data to project that "when today's young adults reach their mid-40s to mid-50s, a record high share (25%) is likely to have never been married" (p. 12).

A critical question is whether people are *choosing* to live single instead of, say, getting stuck with a status they never wanted because of economic challenges, unfavorable marriage markets, or other externalities. In a study in which a representative sample of single Americans were asked whether they were in a committed relationship and whether they were looking for a partner, the biggest group, 55%, said that they were neither in such a relationship nor looking to be in one (Rainie & Madden, 2006). In another national sample (Taylor, 2010), Americans who were not married were asked whether they wanted to get married. Possible responses were yes, no, and don't know. Among those who had always been single, 58% said yes. Among the previously married, just 22% said yes.

I believe there are single people who do more than choose single life – they embrace it. I call them "single at heart" (DePaulo, 2014). By living single, people who are single at heart are living their best, most authentic, and most meaningful lives. Although my research on the topic is just preliminary, a pilot study (DePaulo, 2012) suggests that people who are single at heart differ from those who are not in extent to which they value solitude, self-sufficiency, and meaningful work. In making major changes, they prefer to make the decision that feels right to them rather than deciding with a partner. When attending social events, they prefer having a range of options (such as going on their own or with friends or not attending at all) to attending nearly always with a partner. Other differences pertain to romantic relationships. For example, people who are single at heart are especially likely to say that they are not all that interested in such relationships, and that when they have been in them, they were especially likely to feel relieved when they ended.

The Ubiquity of Claims that Marriage Improves People's Lives

Daniel Gilbert, who has won numerous prestigious awards for his research on happiness, gave a talk on the topic in 2013 to a packed room at Harvard's Peabody Museum. He asked the audience members to raise their hands if they thought that marriage leads to happiness. Addressing a man whose hand was up, Gilbert declared, "You're right." Continuing to use causal language, he said that on average, marriage "makes you happier for eight to 15 years" (Leddy, 2013).

Dan Buettner, another *New York Times* bestselling author who writes about happiness, described what he believes to be some of the most important "steps to improve our happiness." One of them was "find your soul mate" (Buettner, 2013, p. 36). His claim appeared in *AARP Magazine*, a publication with a circulation of well over 20 million.

In 2000, sociologist Linda Waite, together with Maggie Gallagher (conservative commentator and past president of the National Organization for Marriage, a group that opposed same-sex marriage), published the *The Case for Marriage: Why Married People Are Happier, Healthier, and Better Off Financially* (Waite & Gallagher, 2000). The book includes stark causal claims, such as "Marriage makes people happier" (p. 77). In *Singled Out* (DePaulo, 2006) and elsewhere (e.g., DePaulo & Morris, 2005), I critiqued those assertions, including more specific claims about the results of particular studies. Nonetheless, the book has been cited in dozens of scholarly journal articles – nearly always uncritically.

Claims about the purported benefits of getting married have made it into high-profile legal decisions. For example, after Californians voted in 2008 for Proposition 8, which banned same-sex marriage, a Federal District Court in San Francisco struck down the ban two years later (Perry v. Schwarzenegger, 2010). The ruling included this claim: "Marriage benefits both spouses by promoting physical and psychological health" (p. 69), followed by seven paragraphs of similarly worded claims.

In the academic literature on marital status, claims about the benefits of marrying are pervasive. Typically, a few studies are cited – or perhaps Waite and Gallagher (2000) is referenced to legitimate the claims – and then the authors move on to speculate as to why getting married is so advantageous or to introduce their new study of the purported benefits of marrying. But what do those studies really demonstrate, when held to the basic standards of acceptable scientific research?

What is the evidence that getting married makes people happier or healthier or better off in any other psychological or interpersonal way? I will take a brief look at some cross-sectional research, then focus primarily on research on transitions from being single to getting married for the first time. I will also consider transitions from marriage to divorce. I will discuss cohabitation, separation, and widowhood in much less detail. Parental status is a separate issue from marital status; my interest here is in the latter. The literature on family structure (e.g. outcomes of children in single parent vs. two-parent families) suffers from many of the same methodological challenges as the research on marital status (see DePaulo, 2006) but that is not the focus of this article.

Multiple Outcomes Over Time: Implications of Getting Married for Happiness, Health, Depression, Self-Esteem, and Social Ties

Most studies of marital status focus on just one outcome variable, or one type of outcome. Too many are cross-sectional. Almost all of them compare only those people who are currently married (or, in longitudinal research, those who get married and stay married) to people who are not married. Perhaps the only exception to all three of these limitations is Musick and Bumpass's (2012) analyses of the first two waves of data from the National Survey of Families and Households (NSFH). Outcome variables were happiness, health, depression, self-esteem, and social ties (contact with parents, time spent with friends, and relationship quality with parents).

The authors began with the adults who were under age 50 and single (not married and not cohabiting) during the first wave of data collection, 1987-1988. By the time of the second wave about six years later, 1992-1994, some had stayed single, others transitioned to cohabitation, and others to marriage – some directly and others after first cohabiting. The authors compared changes in each of the outcome variables for each of the groups making a transition to the changes for those who stayed single. The single group did not just include those who had always been single; previously married people who were not cohabiting were also included. That is important, since research sometimes shows less favorable outcomes among the previously married than among the currently married or the always-single (e.g., DePaulo, 2006; DePaulo & Morris, 2005; Rook & Zettel, 2005).

Previous research has documented decreases over time in the quality of marital and cohabiting relationships (e.g., Brown, 2003; Umberson, Williams, Powers, Chen, & Campbell, 2005), as well as a honeymoon effect for well-being, such that people who marry experience an initial increase that soon dissipates (e.g., Lucas, Clark, Georgellis, & Diener, 2003). To test for possible differences in outcomes for earlier vs. later years of unions (marriage or cohabitation), Musick and Bumpass (2012) looked separately at recent unions (formed within the previous 3 years) and older ones (formed within the previous 4-6 years).

The authors first reported the usual analyses, in which only those people who got married (or began cohabiting) and stayed together were included. In these analyses, biased in favor of marriage because of the exclusion of all those people who got married but did not stay that way, and because of the inclusion of the previously married with the always-single, the authors found that: (1) there were no differences in health – i.e., people who got married, either directly or after cohabiting, did not become any healthier over time than did the people who stayed single; there were no differences in (2) self-esteem or in (3) quality of relationships with parents; people who got married did become (4) happier and (5) less depressed; people who married, either directly or after cohabiting, (6) had less contact with their parents and (7) spent less time with their friends. The findings for social ties are consistent with previous cross-sectional studies of nationally representative samples (Gerstel, 2011; Gerstel & Sarkisian, 2006); in that research, people who have always been single were most likely to contact, visit, advise, and support their parents and siblings, and the currently-married were least likely to do so. Singles were also the most likely to help, encourage, and socialize with their friends and neighbors.

In the analyses in which all those who got married were included in the married group, even if their union dissolved, and in which the changes over all six years were considered together (rather than broken down into the more recent vs. older unions), people who got married (without first cohabiting) became no happier, no healthier, and showed no greater increases in self-esteem than those who stayed single; the quality of their relationships with their parents was not different either. Only on the depression measure did the married group fare better. The married group did worse with regard to social ties: over time, they had less contact with their parents and spent less time with their friends than did those who stayed single. Those who transitioned from cohabiting to marrying showed no greater improvements in health or self-esteem than those who stayed single; they did become happier and less depressed. Again, they fared worse than the singles with regard to staying in touch with their parents and spending time with friends.

Separate analyses of the more recent unions and the older ones showed that the short-term implications of marrying were positive for some outcomes: Those who had married (or transitioned into cohabitation) within the previous three years were happier, healthier, less depressed, and had higher self-esteem than those who stayed single. There were no differences in the quality of relationships with parents. Those who got married again fared worse on social ties: Over time, they had less contact with their parents and spent less time with their friends.

Any positive outcomes of marrying that show up after just a few years could be just honeymoon effects. Do the positive outcomes endure, and do the negative ones dissipate? In the analyses of the more enduring unions, the authors found that when those who had married (or transitioned into cohabitation) between four and six years ago were compared to those who stayed single, there were *no differences in happiness, health, depression, self-esteem, or relationship quality with parents;* the only significant effects favored single people: they had more contact with their parents and spent more time with their friends.

In the analyses showing some results favoring married people, none of the effects were large. The authors noted that the largest of all of the effects (regardless of which group they favored) were about one-third of a standard deviation and that most effects were smaller. For example, in the analyses including all people who got married (and not broken down by more recent vs. more enduring unions), there were only three significant effects favoring those who married. The decrease in depression for those who married directly was just .12 standard deviations; the increase in happiness and decrease in depression for those who married after cohabiting were both .25 standard deviations.

Getting Married and (Not) Getting Happier, More Satisfied, or Less Depressed

Cross-sectional studies of happiness, life satisfaction, and other measures of subjective well-being are sometimes cited in support of the claim that married people are happier. For example, in a national sample of adults who rated their happiness on a 1-4 point scale, with higher numbers indicating greater happiness, mean happiness ratings were 3.3 for the currently married, 3.2 for the always-single, and 2.9 for both the divorced and the widowed (Gove & Shin, 1989). As is typical, the married group excludes all those people who got married but did not stay that way. Even with that advantage accorded to the married group, the lowest levels of happiness were reported not by those people who had stayed single but instead by those who were previously married. With regard to the question of whether getting married improves happiness (which can only be addressed in the most suggestive way by cross-sectional data), the most relevant comparison is between all people who had ever married and those who stayed single. I have never seen such a comparison reported in a cross-sectional study. It is a straightforward matter to compute the weighted means, though, and in this study, they are the same, 3.2 for both groups.

Over time, the more methodologically sophisticated longitudinal studies have become much more commonplace. Some are prospective studies, in which well-being is assessed repeatedly, beginning before the wedding and continuing for years afterwards. In a meta-analytic review, Luhmann and her colleagues (2012) analyzed 18 independent samples in which the measures of subjective well-being included cognitive well-being (e.g., ratings of life satisfaction), affective well-being (e.g., ratings of happiness or depressed mood), and relationship satisfaction. (The Musick & Bumpass study, with just two data points several years apart, was not included.) On the average, there were 5 assessments and the first was taken an average of four months before the wedding.

Studies of cognitive well-being showed that ratings of life satisfaction were significantly higher just after the wedding than they were before. Over time, though, life satisfaction continued to decline until it was no greater than it was the first time it was measured, when the participants were single. This is the familiar pattern known as the honeymoon effect. The three studies of affective well-being found no effect at all of getting married – there was no honeymoon effect and no subsequent changes in happiness or depressed mood. Studies of relationship satisfaction found that those assessments were more negative just after the wedding than they were before, and they continued to decline over time. Another 20 independent samples of post hoc research (in which the first assessment was not made until just after the wedding) also showed that relationship satisfaction decreased continuously over time.

Some of the studies in the meta-analysis were designed to test the set-point theory of adaptation to life events, and for that reason included only those people who got married for the first time and stayed married over the course of the study. A better test of the implications of getting married for happiness or depressed mood or life satisfaction is offered by those few studies in which people were included in the analyses even if they did not stay married. Results of those studies were not reported separately but they were compared to the results of the studies in which included only those people who stayed married. The decline in subjective well-being in the years after the wedding was even greater for the more inclusive studies than it was for those including only people who stayed married.

The meta-analytic results are not very supportive of claims that getting married makes people happy. Affective well-being, including happiness and depressed mood, showed no improvement at all, not even a short-lived honeymoon effect, and relationship satisfaction, on the average, went nowhere but down. Only life satisfaction increased initially, and that effect did not last. It dissipated especially quickly in studies in which everyone who got married was included, even if they did not stay married.

Was there some way that researchers could still claim that marriage mattered in a positive way? One approach that has been used is to estimate the levels of well-being that participants would have experienced if they had stayed single instead of marrying. In an analysis of British data, Yap, Anusic, and Lucas (2012) found in their normative analyses that both single and married people reported life satisfaction ratings that decreased every year. Those who got married and stayed married, they found, had higher ratings than they would have if they had stayed single. As the authors explained, "...although our previous analyses showed that people were no happier after marriage than they were before, these results suggest that married people are indeed happier than they would have been if they did not get married. This is because if they did not get married their life satisfaction would have decreased even more due to normative declines in life satisfaction common to both married and single groups" (p. 484). (See also Anusic, Yap, & Lucas, 2014a and 2014b, for similar analyses of datasets from Australia and Switzerland.)

> *The meta-analytic results are not very supportive of claims that getting married makes people happy. Affective well-being, including happiness and depressed mood, showed no improvement at all, not even a short-lived honeymoon effect, and relationship satisfaction, on the average, went nowhere but down. Only life satisfaction increased initially, and that effect did not last. It dissipated especially quickly in studies in which everyone who got married was included, even if they did not stay married.*

One problem with this conclusion about people who got married is that it is based on a sample of only those people who got married and stayed married. So we can't say, on the basis of that analysis alone, that "married people are indeed happier than they would have been if they did not get married." But what if we limit the claim to people who got married and stayed married? Then can we say that getting married made them happier?

The people who got married and stayed married are different people than the ones who stayed single, so we don't really know whether they would have been less satisfied with their lives if they stayed single. Maybe they are the kinds of people who would have resisted the usual declines in life satisfaction even if they had not married. But suppose the authors are correct in their suggestion that the people who got married and stayed married were more satisfied than they would have been if they stayed single. What does that mean for the key causal question at the heart of this article – does getting married make people happier or more satisfied? If the people who stayed single had instead married, would they have become more satisfied with their lives?

Remember that the people who got married *chose* to do so. What about the people who stayed single? From national surveys, we know that substantial numbers of people are choosing to live single (Rainie & Madden, 2006; Taylor, 2010). Maybe some are not just choosing single life but eagerly embracing it (DePaulo, 2014). Can we really assume that if those people had been nudged or forced or randomly assigned to marry that they would have become more satisfied with their lives?

Getting Married and (Not) Getting Healthier

An example of cross-sectional research on marital status and health is the National Health Interview Survey, in which a different representative sample of adults in the U.S. was questioned every year beginning in 1972. They self-reported their health as poor, fair, good, or very good/excellent. Liu and Umberson (2008) analyzed marital status differences through 2003. Their dependent variable was not mean health scores but the predicted probability that people in a particular group reported health that was good or excellent.

Remember that the people who got married chose to do so. What about the people who stayed single? From national surveys, we know that substantial numbers of people are choosing to live single (Rainie & Madden, 2006; Taylor, 2010). Maybe some are not just choosing single life but eagerly embracing it (DePaulo, 2014). Can we really assume that if those people had been nudged or forced or randomly assigned to marry that they would have become more satisfied with their lives?

The authors compared five marital status groups – currently married, always-single, separated, divorced, and widowed – overall, and then separately by gender and by race (African-Americans vs. non-Hispanic whites). They found that "the married remain more likely than any other group to report good health for both men and women over the entire study period." They also showed that over time, the difference between the always-single and the currently-married steadily decreased, while the difference between the currently-married and each of other groups (separated, divorced, and widowed) actually increased over time.

The study generated plenty of press, including, for example, the *Washington Post* headline, "Married Folks Still the Healthiest" (Gordon, 2008). Readers might think the lesson is that if they want to be healthy, they should get married. Of course, for all of the usual reasons, that inference cannot be drawn from the research. The married group consisted not of everyone who ever married, but only those who were currently married. Those who got married and then got unmarried reported worse health than those who were currently married; for at least the last 15 years of data, they also reported worse health than those who stayed single. This pattern, in which the always-single people fare most similarly to the currently-married, and the previously married fare the worst, is the same pattern often found in cross-sectional research on happiness. In their review of various measures of physical health, Rook and Zettel (2005) came to the same conclusions. (See also DePaulo, 2006, for a review of many different health measures from CDC data.)

In their review articles, their introductions to empirical articles, and in their summaries in textbooks, authors may be tempted to grab onto the statement of the superiority of the currently-married group over all the others. Let's consider the specifics of those differences for the most recent year for which the data were analyzed, 2003. The probability of reporting good or excellent health for the currently married was .929 (see the graph on p. 246). For those who had always been single, it was .926. Remember that the currently-married group is already advantaged because those who married and then got unmarried have been removed. Even so, their health advantage over all those who stayed single was the difference between .929 and .926.

Among African-Americans, not even that tiny difference appeared; in 2003, the health of the African-Americans who had always been single was identical to the currently-married. With regard to gender differences, a comparison of the separate graphs for women and men (across race) shows that in 2003, the women who had always been single reported better heath than the men who were currently married.

Liu and Umberson (2008) ended their article with an important note of caution: "encouraging marriage in order to promote health may be misguided. In fact, getting married increases one's risk for eventual marital dissolution, and marital dissolution seems to be worse for self-rated health now than at any point in the past three decades" (p. 252).

As indicated in the previous section, the research literature on the implications of marrying for subjective well-being includes many longitudinal studies with numerous waves of assessment. The same is not true of the literature on physical health. Some of the studies compared the same people at just two different points in time. Still, compared to the cross-sectional research, the available studies allow for stronger inferences about the health implications of marrying.

In one example, Williams and Umberson (2004) analyzed data from a nationally representative sample of Americans 24 and older surveyed between 1986 and 1994. They rated their health on a 5-point scale. The authors created a dependent variable that was the predicted probability of reporting excellent or very good health (the top two of the 5 points). When single people who got married (for the first time) were compared to single people who stayed single, the men – but not the women – reported significantly better health. When those who were single throughout the course of the study were compared to those who were married the whole time, there were no differences at all in health for either the men or the women. Overall, those who got divorced were more likely to report improvements in their health relative to those who stayed married. For men, age mattered: health improved for younger men who divorced, but it got worse for older men. For women, getting divorced did not compromise their health at any age.

In another example, Wu and Hart (2002) analyzed two-year intervals of longitudinal data from a representative sample of Canadians between 20 and 64. Their physical health measures were an index of overall functional health (dexterity, mobility, vision, hearing, speech, cognition, emotion, and pain and discomfort) and a self-report of health status. They found that single people who got married reported no better health on either measure than the people who stayed single; the results were true of both the men and the women. Something else was true for both the men and the women: Those who stayed married over the two-year intervals reported significantly *worse* health on both measures than those who stayed single. Men who got divorced reported worse health on both measures than men who stayed single; for women, there were no differences.

So does getting married make people healthier? None of the studies we can conduct in an ethical way would allow us to answer that question in the strongest way possible, methodologically. The evidence available from the studies that have been done provides a tangle of non-results and qualified effects. Cross-sectional comparisons that advantage married people by including only the currently married in the group sometimes show only the tiniest differences between that group and the always-single group, or, in certain comparisons (such as with African Americans), no differences at all (Liu & Umberson, 2008; Rook & Zettel, 2005). The divorced group – people who did get married at one time – typically have worse health than people who stay single, a difference that appears to be increasing over time (Liu & Umberson, 2008). Comparisons over time show that single people who get married (either directly or after cohabiting) show either no improvements in health (Musick & Bumpass, 2012), or improvements only for the men (Williams & Umberson, 2004), or improvements only for the first few years and only if those who transitioned to cohabiting relationships and stayed in those relationships are included in the analyses (Musick & Bumpass, 2012). Comparisons of those who have settled into their marital statuses are even more troublesome for the "get married, get healthy" hypothesis: those who stay married for years are either no healthier (Williams & Umberson, 2004) or less healthy (Wu & Hart, 2002) than those who stay single.

There are many other studies of marital status and health. From just this brief sampling of some of the best, though, it already seems clear that getting married is no surefire path to better health, and should not be described as such.

Getting Married and (Not) Living Longer

To study the implications of getting married for outcomes such as health or happiness, it is possible to follow the same people over time, assessing them year after year. That way, we can see what happens when, for example, people transition from being single to married, or married to divorced. We can track experiences (health, happiness, etc.) leading up to the event, around the time of the event, and in the years afterwards. It is from those kinds of studies that we have seen that any positive implications of marrying sometimes amount to little more than a short-lived honeymoon effect.

When the outcome of interest is mortality, though, the analytic possibilities are more limited. Since death is a one-time thing, we cannot track people's rate of dying as they stay single or get married or get divorced. Brockman and Klein (2004), however, have used the German panel study (ongoing since 1984) to estimate how marital biography might predict mortality. Because the study is so large and has been going on for so long, enough people have died to make mortality estimates possible.

Beginning with cross-sectional analyses, the authors compared the relative mortality risks of the currently single, divorced, and widowed people to the currently married. The married group, therefore, does not include anyone who ever married but only those who are currently married. Their measure was a hazard ratio, indicating the relative risk of mortality for the group in question as compared to the reference group. (Values greater than 1.0 indicate a greater relative risk of dying relative to the reference group, whereas values lower than 1.0 indicate a smaller risk.) The findings did not spell uniform doom for single people. Once selection effects were controlled, the mortality risk for the single men was no different than for the currently-married men. The divorced men had a marginally higher risk than the currently married men. For the women, the currently single did have a higher risk but the divorced women's mortality risk was no different from that of the currently married women.

Next the authors asked whether mortality risks might change over time – for example, as people stay married longer or as more years pass since they divorced. In a key table (Table 3, p. 577), the authors showed the hazard ratios for men and women who had been married (for the first time) for 0-2 years, 2-7 years, and more than 7 years. They also showed the hazard ratios separately for men and women who had been divorced (for the first time) for 0-2 years, 2-7 years, and more than 7 years. The reference group was same-aged people who had stayed single. Again, they controlled for selection effects. The biggest hazard ratio – i.e., the greatest risk of dying – occurred during the first two years of marriage. For men, it was 3.10 and for women, it was 2.44. Getting married seems to more than double or triple the mortality risk during the first two years, compared to staying single. After the second year, none of the effects were significant for the men or the women – the relative mortality risk did not differ from 1.0. Getting divorced also mattered in a negative way at first – in the first two years, it more than doubled the mortality risk for men (2.33) and for women (2.32) compared to staying single. The effect of divorce also dissipated over time. For men, it was no longer significant between 2-7 years after the divorce, or beyond 7 years. For women, it was no longer significant after 7 years; between 2 and 7 years, mortality risk was significantly lower.

In an American longitudinal study, nearly 300,000 people who were at least 45 years old at the start of the study were tracked for up to 11 years (Johnson, Backlund, Sorlie, & Loveless, 2000). The familiar comparisons were used – those who were divorced, widowed, or had always been single at the start of the study were compared to those who were currently married. The abstract made the results seem straightforward: "Each of the non-married categories show elevated RR of death compared to married persons..." (RR is relative risk.) But were all of the unmarried groups really more likely to die younger than the married group?

The authors computed mortality risk for eight different groups: men and women who were Black or White, and, when first assessed, were either between 45 and 64 or 65 and older. Looking first at the people who had always been single, their mortality risk did not differ from the currently-married in three of the four groups of Blacks. (The exception was the younger Black men.) For whites, the always-single groups did have higher mortality risks than the currently-married group. Now let's look at the eight divorced groups. Seven of them have a significantly higher mortality risk than the currently married. (Older Black men were the exception.) Now let's compare the mortality risk (relative to the currently married) of the always-single and the divorced. In seven of the eight comparisons, the divorced had the same or higher mortality risks than the always-single. (Younger white single women had a slightly higher mortality risk than the young white divorced women.)

Does the American study show that if you get married, you will live longer? Not if you are a Black woman or an older Black man. Not if you get married and then get divorced (unless you are an older Black man). Suppose that every comparison of the always-single to the currently married had favored the currently-married people. Then could we say that getting married makes people live longer? Again, no, because in 7 of the 8 groups, the people who married and then divorced did not live longer. Even if everyone who ever got married (and not just the currently married) lived longer than those who stayed single, we could not know for sure that if the single people had married, they would have lived longer. They were different people than the ones who chose to marry.

There are many studies of marital status and mortality. One after another compares only a select group of people who got married to all of the people who stayed single. Those who got married and then got unmarried are excluded from the married group, thereby biasing the results in favor of marriage. Even with that advantage afforded to the married group, the always-single people do not always have higher mortality rates.

Results of a longitudinal study showed that those who had been married for at least four years were not doing any better in any way than those who had stayed single. They were no happier, healthier, or less depressed, and they had no higher self-esteem. They did, though, have less contact with their parents and friends.

Conclusions

Does getting married make people happier or healthier or better off in any other social or psychological way? Because we cannot randomly assign people to marital statuses, we can never answer that causal question in a definitive way. Causal claims about marriage "making" people happier or healthier should not be made in the media, and of course, they should not appear in scholarly publications.

Keeping in mind that the conclusions we draw from the research we can do on the implications of marrying can only be described as suggestive and not definitive, what does the available research suggest? In the media and in scientific publications, claims that getting married is beneficial are rampant. But what do the data actually suggest? One of the most common approaches to the study of the implications of marrying is a cross-sectional one, in which people who are currently married are compared to other unmarried groups such as people who are divorced or widowed or have always been single. As an answer to the question of whether getting married makes people better off, such comparisons give an unfair and scientifically indefensible advantage to the married group, which includes not all people who ever got married – the appropriate group to use to answer the question of whether getting married will make you better off – but only those who got married and stayed married. Since the divorced group often fares worse than the currently-married group – *and* worse than the group of people who have always been single, the common decision to remove them from the marriage group is particularly egregious.

And yet, even though the deck is stacked in favor of the currently-married group in such research, that group still does not fare all that well in comparison to the always-single group. Differences favoring the currently-married group are sometimes tiny. Sometimes they depend on whether the people in question are male or female, Black or white, or younger or older.

Increasingly, studies of the implications of marrying are longitudinal, and those designs allow stronger inferences than cross-sectional designs. Still, in the vast majority of the studies of lives over time, the same biased comparisons are used. The married group typically consists of only those people who got married (often for the first time) and stayed married over the course of the study, and that group is compared to other not-married groups. Such comparisons are never the most appropriate ones if the goal is to answer the question of whether getting married improves people's lives. Yet even when such an unfair advantage is accorded to the married group, the results provide at best a muddled answer to the question.

In some ways, people who stay single do better than those who marry. For example, they have more contact with their friends and their parents. Sometimes getting married results in no benefits at all compared to staying single – for example, there may be no boost to self-esteem, health, happiness, or depressed mood. When getting married does result in improvements relative to staying single, those findings are often not generalizable across groups but instead depend on whether the people in question are male or female, Black or white, younger or older, and whether the people who got married have been married for just a few years or for longer. Longitudinal studies comparing people who remain in their particular marital status over time also fail to support claims about the benefits of marriage: those who stay married do no better, or sometimes even worse, than those who stay single.

The more appropriate analyses, in which all those people who ever married are compared to those who stay single, are rare. Results of such analyses suggest that any findings favoring people who get married become weaker or disappear entirely. For example, Musick and Bumpass (2012) found that those who had been married between four and six years were not doing any better in any way than those who had stayed single. They were no happier, healthier, or less depressed, and they had no higher self-esteem. They did, though, have less contact with their parents and friends.

The studies I reviewed are a selected subset, chosen to illustrate my points using studies that have often been cited in the literature, or studies that are particularly strong (for example, because they are longitudinal, based on representative national samples, or include an array of measures). If I had reviewed more studies, I would have needed to add even more qualifications to the claim that getting married improves people's lives (DePaulo, 2011a). For example, in a study of depression, Frech and Williams (2007) compared only those who got married and stayed married to those who stayed single. They found that those who got married became less depressed than those who stayed single if the focus was on the 20 percent of the people who were already depressed before they got married, or if it was on those who, once married, experienced greater than average marital happiness.

When researchers exclude from the married group those who got married but did not stay that way, sometimes they acknowledge their decision and its implications. For example, in a longitudinal test of "the assumption that marriage enhances well-being" (p. 895), Horwitz, White, and Howell-White (1996) excluded from their sample people who got married and then separated or divorced. "We do not include this group," they explained, "because they clearly are not deriving any benefits of marriage" (p. 899).

There are other ways, too, that researchers advantage the married group in ways that would not be acceptable in research on any other topic. For example, when Hawkley and her colleagues (2008) found no differences in loneliness between currently-married people and currently unmarried people, they then compared to all of the unmarried people just those married people who considered their spouse to be a confidant. Apparently, neither the editor nor any of the reviewers noted that the married and unmarried groups were no longer comparable, as they might be if, for instance, the single group included only those unmarried people who considered their closest friend or relative to be a confidant. More generally, the claim is sometimes made that it is not marriage that is beneficial, but "healthy marriages" or happy ones (e.g., Parker-Pope, 2010). Perhaps this is the rationale for including only the happiest or healthiest couples in the married group, and comparing them to all single people, regardless of their health or happiness. As social scientists, we should question such practices. None of us, for example, would recommend publication of a study in which the manufacturer of a weight-loss drug compared people on their drug who were also exercising to people on the competing drug, regardless of whether they were exercising.

We are left with the insurmountable methodological obstacle we started with: People cannot be randomly assigned to marital status. They get to choose. We just don't know whether people who choose to stay single would have fared better if they were randomly assigned to marry; the marriage data is based on different data — data from people who chose to marry.

The tradition of comparing only those people who are currently married to various groups of currently-unmarried people (either separately or combined, either in cross-sectional or longitudinal designs) is so much a part of the literature on marital status that, sadly, I expect it to continue. Those scholars who do continue to make statements about how the currently married compare to other groups should also address another question: "And so?" Imagine, for example, that a study finds that currently married people are faring better in some way than people who have always been single (or people who are divorced or widowed or separated). What is the answer to the question, "And so?" Is it that the unmarried people should get married? No, because the currently married group does not include all of the people who ever got married. Does it mean that the unmarried group should get married and stay married? We can't say that either. Suppose all those people in intensely hostile, conflict-ridden, and sometimes even abusive marriages had stayed married instead of divorcing: Do we know that they then would have been better off? No, we don't. Then is the answer to the "So what" question that the unmarried group should continue to marry and divorce, marry and divorce, until they find a marriage that makes them happy and healthy? But then what about the potentially adverse effects of all of those transitions?

Suppose, then, that researchers begin to compare all those who ever married to those who stayed single. If they then find that the ever-married group fares better than the ever-single group, does that mean that single people should get married if they want the same benefit? It is a far better design than the one in which only those who got married and stayed married are skimmed off the top of the ever-married group. Still, we are left with the insurmountable methodological obstacle we started with: People cannot be randomly assigned to marital status. They get to choose. We just don't know whether people who *choose* to stay single would have fared better if they were randomly assigned to marry; the marriage data is based on different data – data from people who *chose* to marry.

> *Have researchers simply assumed, consistent with the Ideology of Marriage and Family (DePaulo & Morris, 2005) that of course just about all single people wish they were married and would fare better if they did marry? If social scientists did a study in which engineers were found to be more satisfied with their lives than poets, would they then conclude that if only the poets became engineers, they would become more satisfied with their lives?*

Have researchers simply assumed, consistent with the Ideology of Marriage and Family (DePaulo & Morris, 2005) that of course just about all single people wish they were married and would fare better if they did marry? If social scientists did a study in which engineers were found to be more satisfied with their lives than poets, would they then conclude that if only the poets became engineers, they would become more satisfied with their lives?

Doesn't the approach I'm suggesting, in which everyone who ever married is compared to those who stay single, make it harder to answer the kinds of questions that have interested marriage researchers? Suppose, for example, we want to learn whether the supposedly greater availability of social support in marriage, relative to single life, is linked to better health outcomes. How can we learn about social support in marriage if we include in the marriage group people who were once married but are currently divorced? They are no longer getting any ongoing social support from their marriages.

Doesn't that justify the longstanding tradition of comparing only those who are currently married to some unmarried group? If you want to make that argument, then you also need to agree with the drug companies who want to make claims for the effectiveness of their drugs based solely on people who choose to take it and to continue to take it, while setting aside 43 percent of the people who tried the drug and refused to continue with it. (I'm using 43 percent as an approximation of the divorce rate [Amato, 2010].) Would you sign your name to a review for the NEJM recommending publication of such a study?

Here is another way to think about it. In a longitudinal study of marital status and health, 10,000 Dutch adults were asked about 13 possible health complaints and 23 chronic conditions. The married participants who reported at least four complaints were at least 1.5 times more likely to be divorced after 4.5 years (the end of the study) and those who reported at least two chronic conditions were twice as likely to be divorced by then (Joung, Van de Mheen, Stronks, van Poppel, & Mackenbach, 1998). That's just one study, of course, but knowing that this is an empirically-demonstrated possibility, do you still want to compare only the people who are currently married to people who are unmarried and then try to figure out what it is about marriage that is "making" people healthier?

Suppose you are not dissuaded by anything I've argued so far. You want to continue to include in the married group only those who got married and stayed married. You think it is fine to set aside the 43 percent who disliked their marital experience so much that they refused to continue to stay married. Then how about if I use the same logic in my studies of single people? I want to know about the health implications of staying single. I decide to exclude from my single group the 43 percent who are least happy with their single lives. That's only fair – it is not as if single people can unilaterally decide to marry the way married people can unilaterally decide to file for divorce. If I submitted a paper to a prestigious journal in which I claimed the health superiority of single people based only on the top 57 percent of single people, would you accept it for publication? Would you recommend acceptance to the least prestigious journal?

The tradition of comparing only those people who are currently married to various groups of currently-unmarried people (either separately or combined, either in cross-sectional or longitudinal designs) is so much a part of the literature on marital status that, sadly, I expect it to continue. Those scholars who do continue to make statements about how the currently married compare to other groups should also address another question: "And so?" Imagine, for example, that a study finds that currently married people are faring better in some way than people who have always been single (or people who are divorced or widowed or separated). What is the answer to the question, "And so?" Is it that the unmarried people should get married? No, because the currently married group does not include all of the people who ever got married. Does it mean that the unmarried group should get married and stay married? We can't say that either. Suppose all those people in intensely hostile, conflict-ridden, and sometimes even abusive marriages had stayed married instead of divorcing: Do we know that they then would have been better off? No, we don't. Then is the answer to the "So what" question that the unmarried group should continue to marry and divorce, marry and divorce, until they find a marriage that makes them happy and healthy? But then what about the potentially adverse effects of all of those transitions?

What Do the Findings Tell Us about the Lives of Single and Married People? Theoretical and Conceptual Issues

The belief that married people are better off than single people is so widespread and so rarely challenged that scholars have gone on to address the next question: Why is it that married people do better? Most explanations are categorized as either "social selection" or "social causation." Social selection is the possibility that people who are, say, happier or healthier are more likely to get married or stay married than are people who are less happy or healthy. This is typically the explanation that researchers want to rule out, so as to find support for the preferred causal hypothesis. If married people were already happier or healthier than single people even before they married, then marriage can't be credited with any better outcomes of the currently-married group. Similarly, if less healthy or less happy people are less likely to stay married, then again, that complicates the case for the claim that it is marriage that is "making" people healthier or happier.

Differences on the outcome measure of interest are the most obvious selection variables to be considered, but any other variable that could account for the differences in outcomes between the various marital status groups are also important. That's why demographic variables such as age, income, and education are so often included as controls in marital status research. But trying to equate the currently-married group to one or more of the non-married groups by statistical controls is never going to be wholly satisfying. Researchers may not even think of all of the possible variables that could be relevant, and even if that were possible, the number of variables that can be simultaneously included in an analysis is limited. Statistical controls fall short of random assignment as a way of ruling out alternatives, and again, random assignment to marital statuses is something we just cannot do. We are inevitably left with different kinds of people – those who chose to marry and those who are single, many of whom chose that status.

The pervasive claims about the benefits of marrying are "social causation" explanations. There are variations in the ways that researchers describe social causation. Lamb, Lee, and DeMars (2003), for example, explain social causation this way: "...married persons benefit directly from their relationships with their spouses, in terms of support, intimacy, caring, companionship, and the financial advantages that come with pooling resources...Marriage also has a buffering effect...by moderating the effects of events or circumstances that would result in lower well-being for unmarried persons" (p. 953).

Other scholars include "social control" among the causal mechanisms that account for why people who marry supposedly become healthier. For example, in a section called "The Virtues of Nagging," Waite and Gallagher (2000) declare: "Wives monitor both their own and their spouse's health habits. Wives not only discourage drinking, smoking, and speeding, but they cook low-fat or low-cholesterol meals, add more fruit and vegetables to the family diet, and encourage regular sleeping habits" (p. 55).

Most social causation explanations point to the resources that married people supposedly have that non-married people do not have. Sometimes a "crisis" perspective is added to the "resource" perspective to explain why divorced people sometimes fare less well than the currently married: "...married persons are healthier than persons who have transitioned out of marriage, because the stress of marital dissolution harms one's health..." (Carr & Springer, 2010).

There are at least four problems with social selection and social causation as the explanations for marital status differences. First, they cannot account for many of the actual research results. Second, they exclude other explanations. Third, the validity of marriage as the key construct has not been adequately established. Fourth, with its lopsided focus on the marital experience and neglect of the experience of single life, the framework is underdeveloped theoretically.

Results that Cannot Be Explained by the Purported Benefits of Marriage

The various components of the social causation hypothesis predict much more consistently positive, powerful, and unqualified effects than we find when we look closely at the available research results. They surely do not predict the results of the studies in which the always-single people fare better than the currently married. For example, if married people are so advantaged by the health-monitoring supposedly provided by their spouse, and all the fruits and vegetables purportedly getting included in all those healthful meals, then why are married people fatter than single people (Brown, Hockey, & Dobson, 2010; CDC, 2004)? Why do single people sometimes report better overall health than married people do (e.g., White, 1992)?

Consider, too, the results of a study of members of the military who were wounded after September 11, 2001 and asked about their physical and mental health in 2011 (Krull & Haugseth, 2012). Four groups were compared: married, divorced, separated, and always-single. The results were straightforward. The wounded warriors who had always been single fared best across a wide range of measures. They were least likely to report emotional or physical health problems that interfered with their work or other regular activities; least likely to have symptoms suggestive of PTSD; least likely to be depressed; least likely to be obese; and best able to bounce back from illness, injury, or hardship. If marriage provides more "support, intimacy, caring, [and] companionship" than single life, along with more buffering from the effects of hardship, and more beneficial social monitoring and control, then how is it possible that the single warriors did better than the married ones in so many ways?

The more sophisticated discussions of social causality allow for marital processes that are not uniformly positive. For example, in their discussion of social control, Carr and Springer (2010) note that "marriage may not necessarily promote good (or squelch bad) health behaviors, because spouses tend to share health behaviors..." (p. 750). Their discussion of psychosocial factors includes the possibility of social strain from conflict and negative behaviors as well as social support. The focus, though, is still on the experiences of married people and not single people.

Beyond Social Selection and Social Causation: Other Explanations

The social selection and social causation explanations of any marital advantages often omit other possibilities that have nothing to do with who gets married or stays married or what happens within a marriage. One of the most important of those alternative explanations is singlism – the stereotyping, stigmatizing, and discrimination against people who are single (DePaulo, 2006, 2011b; DePaulo & Morris, 2005). Perceptions of single people are harsher than those of married or coupled people, even in studies in which single and married people are described identically except for their marital status (e.g., DePaulo & Morris, 2006; Greitemeyer, 2009). In a random sample survey of American adults, those who had always been single were much more likely that married people to report discriminatory treatment in informal interpersonal exchanges (Byrne & Carr, 2005). Single people are also targets of discrimination in the housing market (Morris, Sinclair, & DePaulo, 2007).

Some accounts of the resources available to married people, mentioned in social causation explanations, note that married people tend to be better off economically, and "to be insured, to have private health insurance, and to retain coverage upon job loss, drawing on their spouse's benefits..." (Carr & Springer, 2010). Those are important points. Left unstated, though, is the role of legal discrimination in producing these marital advantages. For example, lifelong single people with no children cannot leave their Social Security benefits to anyone else (they go back into the system), and no one else can will their Social Security benefits to lifelong single people. That's just one of the more than 1,000 federal statutes that benefit and protect only those who are legally married (Polikoff, 2008). In fact, the quest for access to these advantages has been one of the motivators of movement to legalize same-sex marriage. Many of these benefits are financial (such as a variety of tax breaks), and can amount to many thousands of dollars over a lifetime (Addo & Lichter, 2013). (Because the transition to getting married can result in significant financial advantages, it is not sufficient, in longitudinal studies, for researchers to control for economic variables only at the first wave of data collection.)

The important people in the lives of single people are left unrecognized and unprotected in other ways, too. For example, under the Family and Medical Leave Act (Family and Medical Leave Act, 1993), eligible employees are entitled to 12 weeks of unpaid leave "to care for the employee's spouse, child, or parent who has a serious health condition" or to deal with "a serious health condition that makes the employee unable to perform the essential functions of his or her job." The married person's spouse is covered under the Act. There is no equivalent person covered for single people. That means that single people cannot take time off under the Act to care for an important person in their life, such as a sibling or close friend; nor can such a person take time to care for them.

The flip side of singlism is important, too. Matrimania is the extreme valuing and celebration of marriage, couples, and weddings that is rampant in popular culture, the media, the workplace, the marketplace, politics, religion, and everyday life (DePaulo, 2006). Single people and single life are not accorded the same value or legitimacy. When people who marry get an initial boost in well-being that then dissipates, perhaps that honeymoon is attributable not (just) to the "support, intimacy, caring, [and] companionship" that they are supposedly getting because of being married, but to the fact that their life choice was just validated by other people, perhaps in a big, expensive celebration of themselves.

Singlism and matrimania pose significant questions for the study of the implications of marrying for health and well-being. For example, if single life were as valued and respected as married life, and if single people had access to the same benefits and protections as married people, how many people would choose to live single? How would the implications of marrying change?

If There Are Relationship Benefits, Can We Really Attribute Them Specifically to Marriage?

As cohabitation continues to grow in popularity, scholars sometimes ask whether the implications of marrying are unique to marriage, or whether they are similar for cohabitation. But adding cohabitation covers only a very limited range of the alternative ways in which the purported benefits of marriage might be obtained. Is it possible that people with one very close platonic friend, compared to people without any such friend, are happier, healthier, less depressed, have higher self-esteem, and live longer? Is it possible that those effects are stronger and less equivocal than the research evidence relevant to marrying? What about a more daring alternative – the possibility that what benefits people's health and well-being, and protects them against the slings and arrows of everyday life, is having not just one special person (whether a partner in marriage, cohabitation, or a close friend) but a network of diverse connections? Perhaps people are more resilient when they look to a number of different people, with different interests and resources, rather than just one significant other? There is, of course, a vast research literature on social support and social networks. What is missing is a sustained research inquiry that places social support networks alongside marriage and cohabitation and compares the implications for health and well-being.

Theoretical Neglect: The Study of Single Life

Single life is not just a place where people mark time until they marry. Many single people are living their lives fully and joyfully. Among relationship researchers and marriage scholars, single people should not just be conceptualized as the comparison group against which marriage is assessed. We need to think more deeply and theorize more seriously about the nature of single life, and especially about the aspects that have been so very neglected for so very long – the experiences of single life that make it so appealing. Once we realize what living single means to people who embrace their single lives, the questions we ask and the outcomes we measure will jump the typical boundaries of health and happiness.

From my pilot studies of people who are single at heart, and from more than a decade of writing for and about singles in the popular press as well as in academic journals, I want to suggest a beginning set of questions that scholars should consider posing in their studies of marital status and single life:

- How close are you to getting the amount of solitude that you desire?
- How close are you to getting the mix of time alone and time together that you consider ideal for you?
- How meaningful is your work? (A longitudinal study – Johnson, 2005 – suggests that single people value meaningful work more than married people do.)
- To what extent do you have a sense of self-determination? (Marks & Lambert, 1998, found that single people fared better than married people on autonomy.)
- To what extent do you have "a sense of continued growth and development as a person" (p. 657)? (Marks & Lambert, 1998, found that single people fared better than married people on personal growth.)
- To what extent are you pursuing your interests and your passions? To what extent are you doing so guiltlessly?
- To what extent can you save or spend your money as you see fit?
- To what extent have you been able to make the life choices that you find most fulfilling and most meaningful?

We also need to ask questions that recognize the ways in which single life is less valued and supported than married life. For example, we can ask single people whether they believe that their close friends are as valued as other people's romantic partners. Are they included in invitations to social events? Do other people ask about them? Do single people find that other important parts of their lives, such as their work, their interests, and their passions, are acknowledged by other people or are single people most often asked if they are seeing anyone?

We should also evaluate the range of competencies that single people have. Some marriage scholars have touted the efficiency that married couples enjoy by their division of labor; even among contemporary couples who embrace less gender-stereotyped divisions, one person might take care of some tasks, while the other specializes in different tasks. That may well have advantages while the union is intact, but what happens when it ends? Do single people – especially those who live alone – develop and maintain more different competencies in more different domains than married people do? Or are they more adept at finding help with the tasks they do not want to do on their own?

Perhaps because scholars have been so sure for so long that getting married makes people better off, they have focused on what they see as the strengths of married life and the risks of single life. We need to generate a more complete psychology. For example, our journals are stuffed with articles on loneliness but include far fewer offerings on the potential benefits of solitude and time alone. The literature on romantic relationship skills and successes is robust, but our understanding of the significance of adult friendship skills is far less developed. Yet, from the little research that is available, we already know that there are ways in which friendship skills are more important than romantic relationship skills (Roisman, Masten, Coatsworth, & Tellegen, 2004). Studies focusing on the relationship between two people in a couple, and no one else, are plentiful, but studies of the potential risks of intensive coupling are far less numerous. Yet there are indications that there could be important vulnerabilities. For example, in their study of different kinds of personal communities, Spencer and Pahl (2006) found that spouse/partner-based personal communities, in which "the partner is the focal point of the person's social world, acting as confidant, provider of emotional and practical support, and constant companion," were associated with lower scores on mental health measures.

Beyond the Question of Who Is Doing Better

One of the defining characteristics of contemporary life in Western societies is the explosion of choices about how to live. In the US, nuclear family households (married parents with dependent children) are outnumbered by households in which people live alone – and have been for years (DePaulo, 2006). Adults no longer need to get married or have children or live in the suburbs or follow any other pre-determined life path in order to live full, satisfying, and meaningful lives. They can choose the path that works for them.

As scholars, we should ask whether individual differences may be more important than we have acknowledged in conditioning the link between relationship or marital status and outcomes. As single life becomes a more viable option, individual preferences and characteristics may become more predictive of the implications of living single rather than getting married (or cohabiting). Already there is some suggestive evidence in support of that hypothesis of a fit between person and relationship/marital status. An example comes from a study of a nationally representative sample of Americans who were 40 and older and had been single their whole lives (Bookwala & Fekete, 2009) and a comparable sample of married people. The role of self-sufficiency differed for the two groups. For single people, the more self-sufficient they were, the less negative affect they experienced. For the currently-married people, the reverse was true: the more self-sufficient among them experienced more negative affect.

Such a research program on fit would acknowledge that people are not randomly assigned to marital status and they never will be. Although not everyone can have the marital status that they choose (some single people wish they were married, and some married people wish they were single even if they do not act on that wish), it is likely that choice has been playing an increasingly important role over time. As people become more free to pursue the way of living that best suits them, and scholars become more evenhanded in the attention they give to different life choices, our understanding of optimal experiences will deepen.

References

Addo, F. R. & Lichter, D. T. (2013). Marriage, marital history, and Black-White wealth differentials among older women. *Journal of Marriage and Family*, *75*, 342-362.

Amato, P. R. (2010). Research on divorce: Continuing trends and new developments. *Journal of Marriage and Family*, *72*, 650-666.

Anusic, I., Yap, S. C. Y., & Lucas, R. E. (2014a). Does personality moderate reaction and adaptation to major life events? Analysis of life satisfaction and affect in an Australian national sample. *Journal of Research in Personality*, *51*, 69-77.

Anusic, I., Yap, S. C. Y., & Lucas, R. E. (2014a). Testing set-point theory in a Swiss national sample: Reaction and adaptation to major life events. *Social Indicators Research*, *119*, 1265-1288.

Bookwala, J., & Fekete, E. (2009). The role of psychological resources in the affective well-being of never-married adults. *Journal of Social and Personal Relationships*, *26*, 411-428.

Brockman, H., and Klein, T. (2004). Love and death in Germany: The marital biography and its effect on mortality. *Journal of Marriage and Family*, *66*, 567-581.

Brown, S. L. (2003). Relationship quality dynamics of cohabiting unions. *Journal of Family Issues*, *24*, 583-601.

Brown, W. J., Hockey, R., & Dobson, A. J. (2010). Effects of having a baby on weight gain. *American Journal of Preventative Medicine*, *38*, 163-170.

Buettner, D. (2013, February/March). Give yourself a happiness makeover. *AARP: The Magazine*, 32-37.

Byrne, A., & Carr, D. (2005). Caught in the cultural lag: The stigma of singlehood. *Psychological Inquiry*, *16*, 84-91.

Carr, D. & Springer, K. W. (2010). Advances in families and health research in the 21st century. *Journal of Marriage and Family*, *72*, 743-761.

Census Bureau News (2014, July 30). Facts for features: Unmarried and Single Americans Week Sept. 21-27, 2014. Retrieved from http://www.census.gov/newsroom/facts-for-features/2014/cb14-ff21.html#.

Centers for Disease Control and Prevention. (2004). Marital status and health: United States, 1999-2002. Advance data, number 351. Hyattsville, MD:National Center for Health Statistics.

Day, M. V., Kay, A. C., Holmes, J. C., & Napier, J. L. (2011). System justification and the defense of committed relationship ideology. *Journal of Personality and Social Psychology*, 101, 291-306.

DePaulo, B. (2006). *Singled out: How singles are stereotyped, stigmatized, and ignored, and still live happily ever after.* New York: St. Martin's Press.

DePaulo, B. (2011a). Living single: Lightening up those dark, dopey myths. In W. R. Cupach and B. H. Spitzberg (Eds.), *The dark side of close relationships II* (pp. 409-439). New York: Routledge.

DePaulo, B. (2011b). *Singlism: What it is, why it matters, and how to stop it*. Charleston, SC: DoubleDoor Books.

DePaulo, B. (2012, May 10). What does it mean to be single at heart? *Psychology Today*. Retrieved from http://www.psychologytoday.com/blog/living-single/201205/what-does-it-mean-be-single-heart.

DePaulo, B. (2014). *The best of single life*. Charleston, SC: DoubleDoor Books.

DePaulo, B. M., & Morris, W. L. (2005). Singles in society and in science. *Psychological Inquiry*, *16*, 57-83.

DePaulo, B. M., & Morris, W. L. (2006). The unrecognized stereotyping and discrimination against singles. *Current Directions in Psychological Science*, *15*, 251-254.

Family and Medical Leave Act of 1993 (1993). The Family and Medical Leave Act of 1993. United States Department of Labor. Retrieved from http://www.dol.gov/whd/regs/statutes/fmla.htm.

Frech, A., & Williams, K. (2007). Depression and the psychological benefits of entering marriage. *Journal of Health and Social Behavior*, *48*, 149-163.

Gerstel, N. (2011). Rethinking families and community: The color, class, and centrality of extended kin ties. *Sociological Forum*, *26*, 1-20.s

Gerstel, N., & Sarkisian, N. (2006). Marriage: The good, the bad, and the greedy. *Contexts*, *5*, 16-21.

Goldstein, J. R., & Kenney, C. T. (2001). Marriage delayed or marriage forgone? New cohort forecasts for first marriage of U. S. women. *American Sociological Review*, *66*, 506-519.

Gordon, S. (2008, August 11). Married folks still the healthiest. *Washington Post*. Retrieved from http://www.washingtonpost.com/wp-dyn/content/article/2008/08/11/AR2008081100632.html.

Gove, W. R., & Shin, H.-C. (1989). The psychological well-being of divorced and widowed men and women. *Journal of Family Issues, 10*, 122-144.

Greitemeyer, T. (2009). Stereotypes of singles: Are singles what we think? *European Journal of Social Psychology, 39*, 368-383.

Hawkley, L. C., Hughes, M. E., Waite, L. J., Masi, C. M., Thisted, R. A., & Cacioppo, J. T. (2008). From social structural factors to perceptions of relationship quality and loneliness: The Chicago Health, Aging, and Social Relations Study. *Journal of Gerontology: Social Sciences, 63B*, S375-384.

Horwitz, A. V., White, H. R., & Howell-White, S. (1996). Becoming married and mental health: A longitudinal study of a cohort of young adults. *Journal of Marriage and the Family, 58*, 895-907.

Johnson, M. K. (2005). Family roles and work values: Processes of selection and change. *Journal of Marriage and Family, 67*, 352-369.

Johnson, N. J., Backlund, E., Sorlie, P. D., & Loveless, C. A. (2000). Marital status and mortality: The National Longitudinal Mortality Study. *Annals of Epidemiology, 10*, 224-238.

Joung, I. M. A., van de Mheen, H. D., Stronks, K., van Poppel, F. W. A., & Mackenbach, J. P. (1998). A longitudinal study of health selection into marital transitions. *Social Science and Medicine, 46*, 425-435.

Krull, H. & Haugseth, M. T. (2012). *Health and economic outcomes in the alumni of the Wounded Warrior Project*. Santa Monica, CA: RAND Corporation.

Lamb, K. A., Lee, G. R., & DeMaris, A. (2003). Union formation and depression: Selection and relationship effects. *Journal of Marriage and Family, 65*, 953-962.

Leddy, C. (2013, February 21). Money, marriage, kids. *Harvard Gazette*. Retrieved from http://news.harvard.edu/gazette/story/2013/02/money-marriage-kids/.

Liu, H., & Umberson, D. (2008). The times they are a changin': Marital status and health differentials from 1972 to 2003. *Journal of Health and Social Behavior, 49*, 239-253.

Lucas, R. E., Clark, A., Georgellis, Y., & Diener, E. (2003). Reexamining adaptation and the set point model of happiness: Reactions to changes in marital status. *Journal of Personality and Social Psychology, 84*, 527-539.

Luhmann, M., Hofmann, W., Eid, M., & Lucas, R. E. (2012). Subjective well-being and adaptation to life events: a meta-analysis. *Journal of Personality and Social Psychology, 102*, 592-615.

Marks, N. F., & Lambert, J. D. (1998). Marital status continuity and change among young and midlife adults: Longitudinal effects on psychological well-being. *Journal of Family Issues, 19*, 652-686.

Morris, W. L., Sinclair, S., & DePaulo, B. M. (2007). No shelter for singles: The perceived legitimacy of marital status discrimination. *Group Processes and Intergroup Relations, 10*, 457-470.

Musick, K., & Bumpass, L. (2012). Reexamining the case for marriage: Union formation and changes in well-being. *Journal of Marriage and Family, 74*, 1-18.

Parker-Pope, T. (2010). *For better: The science of a good marriage*. New York: Dutton Adult.

Perry v. Schwarzenegger (2010). 704 F. Supp. 2d 921 (Dist. Court, ND California 2010).

Polikoff, N. D. (2008). *Beyond (straight and gay) marriage: Valuing all families under the law.* Boston, MA: Beacon Press.

Rainie, L., & Malden, M. (2006). Romance in America. Pew Internet and American Life Program. www.PewInternet.org http://pewresearch.org/pubs/1/not-looking-for-love, Retrieved September 4, 2009.

Roisman, G. I., Masten, A. S., Coatsworth, J. D., & Tellegen, A. (2004). Salient and emerging developmental tasks in the transition to adulthood. *Child Development, 75*, 123-133.

Rook, K. S., & Zettel, L. A. (2005). The purported benefits of marriage viewed through the lens of physical health. *Psychological Inquiry, 16*, 116-121.

Spencer, L., & Pahl, R. (2006). *Rethinking friendship: Hidden solidarities today.* Princeton, NJ: Princeton University Press.

Taylor, P. (2010). *The decline of marriage and rise of new families.* Pew Research Center.

Umberson, D., Williams, K., Powers, D. A., Chen, M. D., & Campbell, A. M. (2005). As good as it gets? A life course perspective on marital quality. *Social Forces, 84*, 493-511.

Waite, L. J., & Gallagher, M. (2000). *The case for marriage: Why married people are happier, healthier, and better off financially.* New York: Doubleday.

Wang, W. & Parker, K. (2014, September). Record share of Americans have never married: as values, economics, and gender patterns change. Washington, D. C.: Pew Research Center's Social and Demographic Trends project.

White, J. M. (1992). Marital status and well-being in Canada. *Journal of Family Issues, 13*, 390-409.

Williams, K., & Umberson, D. (2004). Marital status, marital transitions, and health: A Gendered life course perspective. *Journal of Health and Social Behavior, 45*, 81-98.

Wu, Z., & Hart, R. (2002). The effects of marital and nonmarital union transition on health. *Journal of Marriage and Family, 64,* 420-432.

Yap, S. C. Y., Anusic, I., and Lucas, R. E. (2012). Does personality moderate reaction and adaptation to major life events? Evidence from the British Household Panel Survey. *Journal of Research in Personality, 46*, 477-488.

PART II

GETTING IT RIGHT

On Getting Married and Not Getting Happier or Healthier or More Connected and Not Getting to Live Longer: What the Research Really Does Show – And Why

3

Why No Study Has Ever Shown that Getting Married Makes You Happier or Healthier: The Brief Version

We believe in marriage more than data

We are a nation of matrimaniacs, and it seems like too many of us just can't get enough of studies claiming that married people win. The latest study claiming that marriage makes you happier hit the *New York Times* (and many other media outlets) and immediately climbed to the number 1 spot on the most-read articles.

The article in question is bolder than most. The authors, Shawn Grover and John Helliwell, know it is challenging to claim that marriage *causes* people to become happier, but they think they can make the case anyway. (By the way, the article is just a working paper—it has not been published in a professional journal, meaning it has not been reviewed by other scholars and deemed worthy of publication.)

Later in this book, I will have more to say about this unpublished working paper and many other similar articles. Here I want to tell you my bottom line about this study and every other study making the same claim, including every study that will ever be done: *No study has ever shown definitively that getting married **causes** people to become happier, and no study ever will.*

Why no study can *ever* show definitively that getting married will make you happier

The current authors—and all the other people who try to make the same kinds of claims—want to compare married people to single people, and if they find that the married people look better in some way (say, they are happier), then conclude that if single people would only get married, they would get happier, too. But there is a big problem that can never be fully surmounted: The married people and the single people are different people. Just because the people who chose to get married got happier (*if* they really did—a key question I will address elsewhere ADD CHPT NUM) does not mean that people who like being single and choose that life would be happier if they instead chose to get married.

Think of it this way: Suppose you found, hypothetically, that people who become accountants are happier than those who become poets. Should all the poets then set their imaginations aside and set up shop as accountants—and expect to become happier as a result? It's ridiculous.

Because married people and single people are different people, *any* way that they are different could account for any differences in happiness (again, if such differences really do exist), meaning that marriage might have nothing whatsoever to do with the happiness differences. For example, maybe the people who get married are already happier even before they marry—in which case marriage may be irrelevant. Or maybe they differ in other ways associated with happiness. For example, because legal marriage comes with a treasure trove of legal and financial benefits, as well as discount rates on just about everything, married people may be less likely to be impoverished and that could make them happier. In that case, it's not the marriage that matters but being able to afford food and clothes and shelter.

The smarter researchers realize these things, and they try to take them into account in this way or that, usually using statistical fixes. But the statistical "controls" are just a way of trying to make the best of an impossible situation. Plus, importantly, no one can think of all of the possible ways in which married and single people might differ that could account for any differences in happiness (or anything else). If they can't think of them, they can't control for them at all. And—this will not surprise readers of this blog—marriage researchers don't consider ways that married and single people differ that reflect positively on single people. I have been reading the research on marital status for nearly two decades, and I don't think I have *ever* seen a researcher acknowledge that some people like their single lives and choose to live single, and for them, getting married would not make them happier no matter how many married people have tried marriage and liked it. (Considering the divorce rate, it is not as many as the matrimaniacs would have us believe.)

Here's why the goal of showing that getting married causes people to be happier is an impossible one to achieve: The gold standard for determining *causal* relationships is a true experiment, in which people are randomly assigned to different conditions. So if you really want to know if getting married causes people to become happier, you need to assign people at random (literally—like picking marital status out of a hat) to get married or stay single, and then randomly assign the married people to stay married or get divorced, or heck, become a widow. If you have enough people in your study, then the people who, by chance, end up married are not going to differ, on the average, in any way from the people assigned to stay single. They are not going to be happier or wealthier or healthier or more sociable or more interested in being married. On the average, they will be the same, and so any differences in their happiness will be due to marriage. And those differences won't necessarily favor those assigned to be married, as is so often assumed by matrimaniacs.

(It's more complicated than that. The groups would be the same at the start of the study, but marriage could still benefit the married people in ways that have nothing to do with the marital relationship itself if, for example, married people got more benefits and protections and more money, and more validation and celebration.)

The two main kinds of studies used to address the question of whether getting married makes you happier are cross-sectional studies, in which people are compared at just one point in time, and longitudinal studies, in which the same people are followed over time. Cross-sectional studies are by far the weaker of the two—it is really a stretch to compare people at just one point in time and then try to declare that the people in one of the groups (say, the married people) are happier *because* they are married. No matter how impressive your statistical gymnastics, you are still dancing around the fact that you just don't know why the two groups differ.

Longitudinal research is better because you can follow the same people over time and see whether, for example, people generally become happier after they get married than they were when they were single. In theory, you don't need to worry about ways in which the single people differ from the married people because they are the same people—you are watching how their happiness changes as they transition from single to married.

In fact, though, it's more complicated than that. When single people get married, they do change in ways that could benefit them but have nothing to do with the marital relationship. For example, they get tons more money in federal benefits, they get lots of consumer deals and discounts, and (if they are going from living alone to living together) they benefit from the economies of scale (e.g., one rent and one set of utilities is split two ways). Maybe if people who get married get happier, it is because they have more disposable income, and not because of, say, their relationship with their spouse.

Or maybe they are happier (*if* they are happier, which I will address in Part 2) because marriage and married people are celebrated, valued, and validated, and single life and single people are stereotyped, stigmatized, discriminated against, marginalized, and often just plain ignored. Maybe if the single life and single people were not targets of all that singlism and had just as much respect as married people and marriage, then it would not matter who did or did not get married. Everyone could choose their own path and happiness would follow. (That's the bottom line of what I really think, though there is no good research that tests it. Some people really are better off married; other people really are better off single—that's how they live their most authentic and meaningful life, despite all the ways in which the deck is stacked against them for living single.)

The other problem with longitudinal studies is that if you want to compare people who get married to people who stay single, you are back to all the same problems you have with cross-sectional research. The people who get married are *different people* than the people who stay single. Just because the people who *choose* to marry become happier (*if* they do) does not mean that people who choose to live single would be happier if they were forced into marrying, or bludgeoned by a posse of deluded and matrimaniacal pundits, reporters, and social scientists into thinking that marriage would make them happier.

[Originally published at the "Living Single" blog at *Psychology Today* on January 9, 2015, as Getting Married Makes You Happier? Again, No, Part 1.]

4

Marriage and Happiness: 18 Long-Term Studies

Getting married does not make you happier

What happens to your happiness and satisfaction with your life in the years following a potentially major life event such as getting married or divorced or having a child or becoming unemployed? Social scientists have been doing a lot of research on that question.

What's Wrong with Most Research on Marriage and Marital Status

More social scientists are beginning to realize what should have been obvious all along – we can't just compare, say, people who are currently married to people who are not married, at one point in time, to understand the implications of getting married. If the currently-married people differ from the other people – in happiness, for example – we cannot conclude that they are different *because* they are married.

People who are married and people who are not married may differ in all sorts of other ways (such as financial resources or experiences of stigma – getting stereotyped, excluded, or discriminated against), and it may be *those* ways, rather than marriage, that accounts for any differences in happiness.

There is another big problem, too, as I have been arguing since writing *Singled Out* and even before. The group of people who are currently married does not include all of the people who ever got married. Divorced and widowed people are separated out of the currently-married group. So if currently married people are happier than other people, you *cannot* say that if the unmarried would only get married, they would be happier, too. The divorced and widowed people *did* get married. If you want to understand the implications of getting married, their experiences have to be included.

The real kicker is that even when marriage is given the utterly unfair and methodologically indefensible advantage of a design in which only the currently married are compared to others, there is still very little difference in happiness, and sometimes the people who did get married and then divorced (or were widowed) are *less* happy than those who stayed single. The results from the nationally representative sample that I described in *Singled Out*, for example, were (on a 1 to 4 scale, with 4 indicated the greatest happiness): 3.3, currently married; 3.2, always-single; 2.9, divorced; 2.9, widowed.

Better Ways to Study the Implications of Marital Status for Happiness, Health, and Everything Else

If you really wanted to know, using the scientific gold standard, whether marrying makes people happier, you would have to randomly assign people to get married or stay single and see what happens. Of course, it is not possible to do that.

The next best thing is to study the same people over the course of their adult lives, and see how their happiness or satisfaction with life changes as they experience various life events. If you want to know the implications of getting married (or, say, getting divorced) for people's happiness, then start asking them about their happiness or satisfaction before the event ever happened, and continue asking them (maybe once a year, though more often might be even better) how they feel long after the event occurred.

In the *Journal of Personality and Social Psychology*, a group of four authors published a statistical analysis and summary (a meta-analysis) of 18 such studies of people who got married and 8 of people who got divorced.

For one of the events, they found that people (on the average) felt a little worse just after the event occurred, then, over time, they reported feeling better and better every time they were asked.

For the other event, people may have felt a bit better right after the event than they had before, though it depended on the particular question you asked. Then, over time, they either felt no differently, or they reported feeling even worse. (Again, the particular question matters, though all of the questions have something to do with happiness or life satisfaction or satisfaction with a partner.)

So which of the results describes the implications of getting married and which describes the implications of getting divorced?

It was the people who got divorced who felt worse at first, but then felt better and better over time. The people who used to be single and then got married (well, *some* of the people who used to be single and then got married – more on that in a moment) felt either a little bit better at first (or their feelings/appraisals did not change or they got a bit worse), and then, over time, their feelings/appraisals either stayed about the same or got worse of time. (If you can access the paper, the relevant graphs are Figures 3 and 4.)

The authors realize that you could look at those timelines of well-being and suggest that: (1) getting divorced makes you happier over time; and (2) getting married does not make you happier and may even make you less happy.

They don't like those interpretations. Taking the marriage findings first, they suggest that people were already becoming happier than usual before they married, in anticipation of the wedding. So when married people start reporting lower satisfaction after the marriage than they did before, they are just going back to the level of satisfaction they felt before a wedding was in the picture.

I don't object to that interpretation. It is entirely possible. As the authors note, you would need to study satisfaction for enough years before the wedding to be more certain that this explanation is a good one.

For divorce, the thinking is similar. Levels of happiness were probably already heading down for people headed to divorce, and so getting divorced only makes people happier relative to how increasingly miserable they were feeling, year after year, when they were married. Again, I buy that as plausible, and related research suggests as much.

The 18 Long-Tem Studies of the Implications of Marrying: Some Specifics

The 18 key studies of the implications of marrying for well-being were all prospective studies. That means that people were asked about their happiness or satisfaction starting *before* they got married and continuing for a while afterwards. On the average, people started reporting their satisfaction about 4 months before they married, and continued doing so repeatedly. The average number of times they reported their satisfaction was about 5. Some of the research has been ongoing for more than a decade.

In at least 11 of the 18 studies, the people in the marriage group included *only those who got married and stayed married* all through the study. This is important. The cumulative results of the 18 studies don't really tell us about the implications of getting married; instead, they tell us about the implications mostly only for those who get married and stay married. For those who marry and then divorce or become widowed, the implications may be very different.

The authors of the 18 studies asked about well-being in at least one of three different ways:

- *Happiness*. I'm calling this happiness, but the authors of the meta-analysis use the term "affective well-being." The participants in the studies were sometimes asked about happiness and sometimes asked about unpleasant feelings such as a depressed mood (which is different from clinical depression).
- *Life satisfaction*. Participants are asked how satisfied they are with their lives. The authors called this "cognitive well-being."
- *Relationship satisfaction*. Participants are asked how satisfied they are with their relationship with their partner.

The first question the authors of the meta-analysis answered was: How did the participants' happiness or satisfaction change from just before they got married to just after? (Remember, "just before" was, on the average, 4 months before the wedding. Just after was the first time they were asked after the wedding.) The second question was: How did happiness or satisfaction change over time after the wedding?

Here's what they found:

- For *happiness*, there was *no difference* in happiness from just before the wedding until just after. Over time, on the average, happiness did not change. Participants did not get either happier or less happy as the years of their marriage marched on.
- *Satisfaction with life* did *increase* from just before the wedding to just after. But then it *decreased* continually over time.
- Compared to life satisfaction, *relationship satisfaction decreased* from just before the wedding to just after. As time went on, relationship satisfaction continued to decrease at about the same rate as overall life satisfaction.

Here's what did *not* happen: Except for that initial short-lived honeymoon effect for life satisfaction, **getting married did *not* result in getting happier or more satisfied**. In fact, for life satisfaction and relationship satisfaction, the trajectories over time headed in the less satisfied direction.

What is really remarkable about the combined findings of the 18 studies is that the designs were biased in favor of making marriage look good. At least 11 of the studies included *only those people who got married and stayed married*.

There was one sentence in the results section of the meta-analysis about how the results were different for those studies which included people who had separated, rather than tossing them out of the marriage group: "These samples did not differ in the initial reaction; however, the rate of adaptation was significantly less negative in samples without any separations."

Translation: Negative adaptation means that people were getting less satisfied over time. If you take out the people who got separated and just look at the people who got married and stayed married, then the decrease in happiness is not as striking. That's another way of saying what I've been saying all along: If you just look at the people who got married and stayed married, you are skimming off the top. You cannot generalize from just those people to offer blanket advice such as, Get married and you will be get happier (as Dan Buettner, author of _The Blue Zones_, actually did in the February/March 2013 issue of the _AARP Magazine_). Even the skimmed people did not get happier and stay happier.

After 18 Failures to Show that Getting Married Increases Happiness, They Are Still Insisting that It Does

Too many social scientists simply are not going to give up on the claim that getting married makes you happier. _Harvard Magazine_ recently reported that Dan Gilbert, Harvard professor and bestselling author of _Stumbling on Happiness_, delighted an audience by asking them "how many believed getting married led to happiness" and then proclaiming "you're right!" to the people who raised their hands.

There were no references in the magazine, but maybe Gilbert was referring to the latest attempt to salvage the myth of marital bliss. It was a study of people's life satisfaction over time, similar to the ones I described above. (It probably was one of the 18 studies, though the specific studies were not listed in the article.)

In the same type of analyses conducted for the 18 studies, participants' reports of their life satisfaction were tracked starting before they married and continuing for years afterwards. Only those who got married and stayed married throughout the study were included in the analyses.

The results were the same as for the 18 studies. Participants reported an increase in life satisfaction around the year of the wedding (compared to before the wedding), but, as the authors noted, "this effect was short-lived." Over time, the participants went back to feeling as satisfied or as unsatisfied as they were with their lives before they got married.

So how did the authors find a way to make getting married look like a boon to happiness? First, they looked at normative changes in life satisfaction over the course of the adult years. Setting aside considerations of marital status, the study showed (as have other studies) that life satisfaction decreases over time. Then they looked specifically at the people who stayed single, and found that their life satisfaction showed some decrease over time.

(Some specifics: At the time of the marriage, those who got married and stayed married reported life satisfaction that was a half of one point, on a 7-point scale, higher than the matched single people. In the years afterwards, those who married and stayed married averaged .28 of one point on a 7-point scale greater life satisfaction than those who stayed single. About the "matching": For each person who got married and stayed married, the authors tried to find a single person who was as similar as possible in age, sex, education and income. They didn't say when they assessed income. The matching was not totally successful. For example, the single people, on the average, were four years older than those who got married and stayed married.)

Here's what the authors said about their results: "…although our previous analyses showed that people were no more happier after marriage than before marriage, these results suggest that married people are indeed happier than they would have been if they did not get married."

That interpretation was repeated in the press. The study may also be the basis for claims by people such as Dan Gilbert that getting married makes you happier.

Do You See What Is Wrong with the Study and the Claims about the Results? If So, You Are Way Ahead of Most Journalists, Professors, and Bestselling Authors

I think there are at least two major problems with the claims made about what this study suggests. The authors of the study acknowledge only one of them. There are also a number of alternative interpretations that go unmentioned.

See if you can figure out the flaws in the study and in the claims made about the results. I'll tell you what I think they are in Chapter 20.

I'm guessing that many of you can identify problems and generate alternative interpretations, even though you may have no training in research methods. If you can, you are doing better than the authors of the study, the reviewers and editors who critiqued the study before it was published, the journalists who wrote about it, and highly successful people such as Harvard professor Dan Gilbert and "happiness expert" Dan Buettner.

[Originally published at the "Living Single" blog at *Psychology Today* on March 15, 2013.]

5

American Marriages: Happiness and Health Decline Over Time

Sometimes people feel better just after marrying, but often that doesn't last

We know about the trajectories of happiness for German and Dutch people who get married and stay married. Longitudinal research (in which the same people are followed for years — in the German study, more than 20 years) has shown that when people marry, those who will stay married enjoy a "honeymoon effect."

They become a bit happier around the time of the marriage, but then that happiness dissipates over time. On the average, the Germans who married and stayed married returned to the same level of happiness they experienced when they were single, and that happened within a few years. The increase in happiness lasted longer for the Dutch.

In my writings on marital status and happiness (in *Singled Out* and elsewhere), I've pointed out that those happiness studies don't really tell us how happiness will change when you marry, because the honeymoon effect occurs only for those who stay married. Those who marry and then divorce actually become a bit less happy as their wedding day approaches and that decline continues until the year before the divorce becomes final.

Individual people approaching marriage do not know which group they will end up in – the one that stays married or the one that gets divorced. If we want to know the implications for happiness (or anything else) of getting married, we need to look at the results for everyone who marries, and not just those who stay married.

At last, there is a longitudinal study in which the data were analyzed in the appropriate way — all people who ever married during the course of the study were compared to those who stayed single. It just appeared online in the February 2012 issue of the *Journal of Marriage and Family*. A national sample of Americans was surveyed in 1987 or1988 and then again six years later, between 1992 and 1994.

Authors Kelly Musick and Larry Bumpass analyzed the data from more than 2,700 adults under the age of 50 who were single and not cohabiting when they were first surveyed. They examined the implications of getting married or cohabiting on not just happiness, but also depression, health, self-esteem, and social ties. In this post, I'll describe the health and well-being of people who become partnered, whether by marrying or cohabiting.

First, the authors repeated the same (or similar) analyses that had been conducted in the German and Dutch studies – they looked only at those people who got married (or started cohabiting) and stayed that way. Because the previous studies showed that any increases in happiness tended to dissipate over time, the authors looked separately at those who became partnered recently (within the past three years) and those who had gotten partnered less recently (between 4 and 6 years ago). In the Dutch study, it took more than 6 years for the happiness levels to return to where they were before the participants got married.

In the American study, some of the dogs just did not bark. People who became partnered did not report any better health than those who stayed single. Those who were partnered recently had not become any healthier and those who had been partnered for a longer time had not become any healthier either.

Those who had gotten partnered within the past three years reported higher self-esteem than those who stayed single. For those who had gotten partnered more than three years ago, though, their self-esteem was no different from those who stayed single.

This select group of people who got partnered and stayed that way did report greater happiness and less depression than those who stayed single. However, those effects were smaller among those who had been partnered for more than 3 years.

Now, at last, the results I've been waiting for all these years: If you include in the analyses all of the people who ever got partnered, how do they compare to those who stayed single? Again, the newness of the union matters. Those who had gotten partnered recently did report better outcomes on all of the measures of psychological well-being. But, for those who had gotten partnered between four and six years ago, there were no differences whatsoever between them and the people who had stayed single.

The bottom line is dramatically different from the mythology about the transformative effects of getting married. If you include everyone who got married or started cohabiting over the course of the six year study – and not just those couples who stayed together – then **those who got partnered between four and six years ago differed not at all from those who stayed single. They were not happier, they were not any less depressed, they were not healthier, and they had no higher self-esteem**.

Now let's all stand back and wait to see whether those findings make headlines.

[Originally published at the "Single at Heart" blog at *PsychCentral* on January 13, 2012.]

6

Wounded Warriors: The Single Ones Are the Most Resilient

You don't see them on TV, rushing into the arms of a spouse, but they are amazing

Do you know the cliché about "the rock"? That's what married people often call their spouse, especially in times of difficulty. In the media, the same sort of story is popular: When one person in a couple seems to be there for their partner, the first person is called "the rock."

Supposedly, the social support that one spouse can give to another is supposed to result in married people being mentally and physically healthier than single people. I have debunked the myth that if you get married, you will get healthier, in *Singled Out*.

Now there are some brand new data, thanks to a RAND report on the Wounded Warrior Project.

Members of the military who were wounded after September 11, 2001 were invited to register for the Project, which is "a not-for-profit organization whose mission is to honor and empower wounded warriors by raising awareness about the needs of injured service members, helping them assist one another, and providing programs that nurture the mind and body and encourage economic empowerment and engagement." Then, in 2010 and again in 2011, the vets were invited to participate in an online survey about their mental and physical health, their education, work status, and home ownership status.

Results were similar for the two years, so here I will report the results for 2011, in which more than twice as many wounded warriors participated (2312 of them) than in the previous year. There were also nearly 500 warriors who participated at both points in time. Those could have been very telling data if the authors had looked at whether the warriors' health (or anything else) had changed as their marital status changed. However, no such analyses were reported.

MENTAL and PHYSICAL HEALTH

Let's consider how the warriors' mental and physical health differed depending on whether they were married, divorced, or had always been single. (Results for the separated were also in the report, but since that group was the smallest, and results were very similar to those for the divorced, I have not included those numbers here.)

Below, I have listed the results for various measures of mental and physical health. There are lots of data, but the bottom line is straightforward: *The wounded warriors who had always been single have the best mental health and physical health.*

Specifically, the warriors who had always been single were:

- Least likely to report emotional problems that interfered with their work or other regular activities
- Least likely to have symptoms suggesting PTSD
- Best able to adapt or bounce back from illness, injury, or hardship
- Least likely to be depressed
- Least likely to report physical health problems that interfered with their work or other regular activities
- Least likely to be obese

Emotional problems interfered with work or other regular activities:
    59%, married
    69%, divorced
    50%, always-single

Has symptoms suggesting PTSD:
    68%, married
    77%, divorced
    61%, always-single

Able to adapt or bounce back from illness, injury, or hardship:
    60%, married
    53%, divorced
    68%, always-single

Probably depressed:
    61%, married
    74%, divorced
    54%, always-single

Physical health problems interfered with work or other regular activities:
    68%, married
    64%, divorced
    51%, always-single

Obese:
    45%, married
    37%, divorced
    33%, always-single

[Originally published at the "Single at Heart" blog at *PsychCentral* on September 9, 2012.]

7

Single Men Have Good Hearts

Why singles have something to get pumped about

Have you heard the one about the wild and unhealthy single men and the better-behaved and healthy-living husbands? It is not a joke (though it should be) - it has been described as scientific fact. The book, *The Case for Marriage*, is full of misstatements and cheater methods that make married people look better than they really are and singles look worse. (These are described in detail in Singled Out.) But, sadly, *The Case* is often cited, so it is a good source of conventional (though dopey) wisdom about the implications of getting married.

The Conventional Wisdom about Getting Married and Getting Healthy

Here are a few choice quotes about single and married men from The Case:

- *"For men, a lot of the health advantages of marriage can be summed up in a single phrase: Fewer stupid bachelor tricks.*
- *"Wives not only discourage drinking, smoking, and speeding, but they cook low-fat or low-cholesterol meals, add more fruits and vegetables to the family diet, and encourage regular sleeping habits."*
- *"When men lose their wives, either to death or divorce, they once again resume their bachelor habits."*

Those poor single men. They must be keeling over from heart attacks and strokes, or waddling into old age with bloated bellies filled with a lifetime of beer and bratwurst. Since it's American Heart Month, I suppose we should pay attention.

Getting Married and Getting Heart Disease: A National Study

I like to fight singlism with science, so I was delighted to discover a report of an 8-year study of heart disease, based on a nationally representative sample of more than 9,000 people in late mid-life. When the study first started in 1992, the participants ranged in age from 51 to 60.

The participants were contacted five times from 1992 and 2000. Their marital status, cardiovascular health status, and health behaviors were assessed. Other information (for example, socioeconomic status) was also recorded.

There are five different marital statuses:

- Continuously married (i.e., first and only marriage)
- Remarried
- Widowed
- Divorced
- Always single

Let's look first at the prevalence of heart disease at the start of the study. (Heart disease = doctor diagnosis of heart attack, coronary heart disease, angina, congestive heart failure, or other heart problems, or stroke.) In the table below is the **percentage of people** (averaged across all ages) **who had heart disease at the start of the study**. Lower numbers indicate less prevalence of heart disease, so the group ranked #1 is the healthiest. The rank-ordering of heart disease for the 5 marital statuses was the same for the men as for the women. See if you can guess which marital status goes with each rank.

	Women	Men
1	8.4	13.0
2	8.7	13.5
3	10.7	16.4
4	10.8	16.5
5	11.6	17.7

Okay, here are the answers:

1. Always single
2. Continuously married
3. Remarried
4. Widowed
5. Divorced

So there you have it. The lowest rate of heart disease is found among the women and men, ages 51-60, who had been single all their lives. The rates for the continuously married are higher, though not statistically so.

The study went on for years, and the authors calculated the probability of experiencing heart disease for each age, from 51 through 65. (See Table 5 in the article.) Of course, the probabilities increase with age for men and women of all marital statuses. Let's see where they end up at age 65. Here are the results for the **MEN**:

1. **29**, always-single men
2. **33**, widowed men
3. **42**, remarried men
4. **46**, continuously married men
5. **50**, divorced men

Look at what has happened to the continuously married men. At 46%, the likelihood of having heart disease is greater for them than for any other group of men except the divorced. The always-single men are doing way better, at just 29%.

(For women at age 65, the probabilities were 32 for continuously married, 38 for always-single, 43 for widowed, 45 for remarried, and 47 for divorced. So even though men typically have higher rates of heart disease than women, the always-single men have the lowest rates of all 10 of the groups.)

The authors also looked at how the risk of heart disease changed for each successive year of marriage. Here, in their words, is what they found: "Each year in marriage increased rather than decreased the risk of cardiovascular disease by 2% for both men and women." The risk increased each year both in first marriages and in remarriages.

Because the authors collected data on health measures such as smoking and obesity, and on conditions described as morbid (really, that's the technical term), they could venture a data-based explanation as to why each year of marriage added to the risk of heart disease: "**Longer marriages were associated with less healthy behaviors and an accumulation of morbid conditions, such as hypertension, diabetes, and high cholesterol.**"

So much for *The Case for Marriage* with its wives preparing low-cholesterol meals for their husbands, with fresh fruit for dessert. (And yes, that book, published in the year 2000, envisions wives making all the meals for their husbands.) And about those "stupid bachelor tricks" - perhaps the authors would like to revisit that claim?

Where Were the Feature Stories about These Findings?

This national study of heart disease was published in a very reputable journal (*Journal of Marriage and Family*) in 2006. Do you remember seeing any headlines about it in the media? I don't either.

Can you imagine how many feature stories you would have seen if the results were reversed, and the continuously married men (rather than the always-single men) had lower rates of heart disease than all of the other men and even all of the other women?

Here's my guess about why the great results for single men did not get much attention: Matrimania sells, and the bashing of single men is in.

Here's another. If you look at the published summary of the article (which you can read here), you will see that the results for the always-single men (or women) are not even mentioned. Instead, the focus is on the bad things that happen to your heart if you "lose" a marriage.

What about the Other Kind of Heart?

By medical measures, always-single men have good hearts. But what about the other sense of a "good heart," the meaning that is more about the kind of person you are than about the condition of your body parts?

I find this an especially interesting question in light of the recent books about single men that seem so demeaning (sometimes unwittingly so). In a conversation about one of those books (*Guyland*), Jeff Arnett told Living Single readers what the research really does show about single men during emerging adulthood:

"What's really striking is how much less sexist, racist, and homophobic young guys are now than in the past. Most want an equal partner in a romantic and sexual relationship, not just someone who will serve them. Most have friends who are of different ethnic groups, and most have gay or lesbian friends and don't make a big deal out of it. What's more, rates of every type of 'guy problem' have declined sharply in the past 30 years among emerging adults-including alcohol use, crime, and unprotected sex. So the assertion that the typical young guy today is a drunken porno-mad potential rapist is nonsense. It's untrue and unfair."

Personally, since Singled Out was published, I've met many single men at my talks and book signings, and - minus the visuals - I've met many more in the e-mails I've received about issues of singlism and living single. I realize my experiences may be unrepresentative and my opinion may be biased, but I'll state it anyway. I believe that most single men have very good hearts.

[Originally published at the "Living Single" blog at *Psychology Today* on February 22, 2009.]

8

Get Married, Get Heart Disease: Study of 3.5 Million Adults

Who really has the healthiest hearts?

Shame on the Associated Press for leading with this: "Love can sometimes break a heart but marriage seems to do it a lot of good." Even more shame on *Time* magazine for cueing up this misleader, soaked in singlism: "Lovelorn singles, that ache in your heart will subside once you get married." (At least they added "sort of" as the next two words.) Really, *Time*, all singles are lovelorn, and you believe everything you read unthinkingly and uncritically?

Double, triple, quadruple shame on the authors, who ended their PowerPoint presentation with this gem, presented as a cutesy cartoon: "Here's the deal: Stay married or put yourself at risk."

The heading of the article you are reading, "Get Married, Get Heart Disease: Study of 3.5 Million Adults," is one way to represent the study that has been making the media rounds, starting, I think, with the Associated Press report and then picked up promiscuously by all sorts of media outlets since then. I don't think my headline is totally accurate, for reasons I will describe. But it is at least as accurate as many of the other claims you may have seen – all of which insisted that Married People Win.

Here's what my claim is based on. In slide 5 of the slide show (appears as a Power Point presentation if you paste this into your browser: timedotcom.files.wordpress.com/2014/03/marital-status-abstract-ppt-presentation-web-briefing-edited1.pptx), you will see the results of a greatly flawed study. One of the cardiovascular diseases they assessed was *coronary heart disease*. In the slide, people who have always been single are the comparison group. The groups compared to them are the currently married, the divorced, and the widowed. *All three groups have higher rates of coronary heart disease than the always-single*. One way to characterize these results is to say that **if you have ever gotten married, you are more likely to have coronary heart disease than if you stayed single**. Again, that's not how I would describe the results of this wholly assailable study – or at least not without qualification. I'm using these headlines to make a point.

Other results seem less promising for single people. For example, the first part of the graph summarizes the results from all vascular diseases. It shows that the currently married have 5% lower odds of having any kind of vascular disease than the always-single. So does that mean, as the AP so irresponsibly put it, that "marriage seems to do it [your heart] a lot of good"? Is *Time* right in stupidly saying that your heart problems will subside "once you get married"? Look at the people who divorced. They got married, and they have a 5.1% greater chance of having any kind of vascular disease than the people who stayed single all their lives.

But none of these claims – not even the ones I like – should be taken seriously. Let me tell you just a few things about this study and I bet the long-time readers of this blog will instantly know what is wrong with each – even if they have no training whatsoever in research. So what excuse do paid writers for AP and *Time* have? What excuse do the authors of the original study have for the claims in their presentation?

What follows are just a few critiques. If you look at the authors' presentation and the reports in the media, you can probably find even more problems.

Fact 1: The study compares currently-married, always-single, divorced, and widowed at one point in time.

The Problem: This is one of the most fundamental flaws of bad research. If you ever took a research methods class, even as a beginning undergraduate, you should have learned this on the first day. In fact, if you ever took a decent class in social psychology or even introductory psychology or any other class in the social sciences, you should have learned this: The study is correlational. **Correlation is not causality**. (How can someone be a social science or health writer for the AP or *Time* magazine and not know something this basic?) *Any way in which the currently married people differ from the single people – other than the fact that they are married – is a possible alternative explanation of why their health differs*.

Fact 2: The study compares the currently-married to the always-single, divorced, and widowed people.

The Problem: This is the classic cheater technique. I critiqued it in detail in _Singled Out_, and I referred to it often in debunking lots of other flawed studies making scientifically irresponsible claims about the implications of getting married for health, happiness, longevity, and more. The authors are skimming the currently married off the top of all of the people who ever got married, then they or others (such as *Time* magazine) are using those findings to suggest what would happen if you, as a single person, got married, or if you, as a married person, stayed married.

But the divorced people got married, too! If you want to talk about the implications of marrying, *you need to include all of the people who ever got married*. Otherwise, you are just cheating. As I've often said before, looking only at the currently married is like a drug company who wants you to evaluate their drug based only on the results of the people for whom the drug worked – when close to half of the people who took the drug got sicker and refused to continue.

About the authors' cutesy cartoon telling married people to stay married or put themselves at risk: Seriously, authors? You think your study shows that if those people who were in horrible, conflict-ridden marriages – maybe even abusive marriages – had stayed married instead of getting divorced, they would be healthier?

If you want to see the implications of marrying or divorcing, you need to follow the same people over time to see how their health or happiness (or anything else that interests you) changes as they go from being single to married or married to unmarried. Even then, you need to look at all the people who ever married, not just those who got married and stayed married. And it still would not be as good as a true experiment that randomly assigns people to different conditions, but we can't assign people to get married or divorced or stay single.

Fact 3: The people who participated in the study were those who sought screening from the company, Life Line Screening.

The Problem: This is not a random or representative sample of Americans. It is not a random or representative sample of single people or married people or divorced people or anyone else. They are people who self-select to get screened by a particular company. (The critique of this company or the kinds of screenings they recommend is beyond my scope here.) Who knows how they differ from everyone else, or what those differences might mean for what we make of the results of the study.

Fact 4: The study is based on more than 3.5 million Americans.

The Problem: The numbers are a red herring. In general, bigger studies are better studies. But if your study is deeply flawed, adding more people does not help. I would not be any more impressed with the results of this study if it were based on 4 billion people or on all of the adults alive in the universe. There was an old saying where I grew up (maybe it is popular everywhere): *"You can't shine sh*t."*

[Originally published at the "Living Single" blog at *Psychology Today* on April 1, 2014.]

9

Men, Women, Single, Married: Who Really Exercises More?

13,000 Americans report their time spent exercising

It is at the top of many people's New Year's resolutions. It is what people vow to do even when the New Year's celebration is a foggy memory. Get more exercise! So who really does get more exercise?

I was especially happy to find the study I'm going to tell you about because exercise is something that comes up not infrequently in the comments posted to this blog. And though I comment on the comments only occasionally, I always read them and stay alert for relevant research that addresses the questions that come up.

The study was based on data collected in the year 2000 from a national sample of more than 13,000 Americans, ages 18 to 64. The study was a cross-sectional one (data were collected at just one point in time) so we need to be cautious in interpreting any marital status differences. A better study would follow the same people as they stay single or marry or divorce or remarry, and see how their patterns of exercise change.

The participants were asked if they engaged in each of 16 different "exercises, sports, or physically active hobbies" or any other type of exercise not listed, during the previous 2 week period. They were also asked how many minutes they spent at each. Adding all of the time spent exercising added up to the averages that are listed below. (The first number is the number of hours and the next two are the number of minutes; so 8:03 is 8 hours and 3 minutes over the course of 2 weeks.)

Time Spent Exercising

Men

       8:03 always single
       6:10 divorced/separated
       4:47 currently married
       5:46 widowed

Women

       5:25 always single
       4:17 divorced/separated
       4:00 currently married
       3:13 widowed

Men get more exercise than women in every marital status category. People who have always been single - including both men and women - get more exercise than people in any other marital status category. The currently married get the least exercise among the men, and next-to-least among the women.

Statistical analyses control for age, so that does not account for the differences.

What's with the married men getting so little exercise relative to all of the other men? I bet you can anticipate the authors' guess about this before they analyzed the data: The married men work harder at their jobs and some of them are spending time as parents, too. The authors tested that, in analyses that controlled for the men's parental status and the number of hours they spent at work. Guess what? Married men still got less exercise than single men.

The authors also tested the prediction that marriage and family status would put a bigger dent in women's exercise time than men's. Again, this study does not allow for an ideal test of that hypothesis, but even in a suggestive way, the data are not cooperating. For men, the difference in exercise time between the always-single and the currently married is a whopping 3 hours and 16 minutes for the 2-week period. For women, it is just 1 hour and 25 minutes.

Here's another interesting (though just suggestive) nugget from the authors:

> *"From the mid-1970s to the mid-1990s, during the period when adult women's labor force participation increased, women's participation in exercise increased dramatically."*

Reference:

Nomaguchi, K. M., & Bianchi, S. M. (2004). Exercise time: Gender differences in the effects of marriage, parenthood, and employment. *Journal of Marriage and Family*, *66*, 413-430.

[Originally published at the "Living Single" blog at *Psychology Today* on January 14, 2011.]

10

The Fragile Spouse and the Resilient Single Person

Is your partner your everything? Is that romantic? Maybe it's risky.

Who are the people who are important to you now? That was the key question that motivated a significant study of the personal communities of people in contemporary Britain.

Think about the question as it applies to your life. The people can be from any categories – family, friends, spouse/partner, coworkers, neighbors, and so forth. You get to define what "important" means.

Using a series of concentric circles, put yourself in the innermost circle, then put the people who are the very most important to you in that same inner circle. Add more people to the other circles in order of their importance to you. Use as many or as few of the circles as you consider relevant.

That's what Liz Spencer and Ray Pahl did in their study. They interviewed, in depth, 60 people in their own homes. The participants ranged in age from 18 to 75, and they were diverse in race, sexual orientation, employment status, marital status, parental status, health, mobility, and living arrangements.

The concentric circles correspond to "personal communities." Most of them fit into one of 7 types. Here's a description of one of the types that may sound familiar, a **partner (spouse)-based personal community**:

> *"The partner is the focal point of the person's social world, acting as confidant, provider of emotional and practical support, and constant companion."*

Not everyone in the study who had a spouse (partner) had a partner-based personal community. For those who did, their partner was in that innermost circle, and no one else shared that space (except, sometimes, for other members of the immediate family). People with partner-based communities often had other family members and friends sprinkled throughout the circles. However, they were not close to their family members and their friendships were narrow (limited, for example, to socializing and not confiding).

I found this partner-based personal community particularly intriguing because it seems to correspond to the type of coupled-relationship that is celebrated, even swooned over, in our society. Consider, for instance, the many songs with lyrics that all sound so similar:

- "You're my everything;"
- "I just want to be your everything;"
- "How can I live without you? You're my world, my heart, my soul."

To many loving listeners, these lyrics are truly romantic. These describe the soulmate they yearn for, or would like to think they already have.

Popular culture is rarely so enthralled by the other 6 types of personal communities. **Family-based** personal communities, in which family is deeply and broadly valued beyond just the nuclear family, do get respect, but not too many chart-topping tunes. **Friend-based** communities are good dramatic television and movie material, until the writers marry off all of the main characters. (Spencer and Pahl describe two different family-based personal communities, and two friend-based communities, varying in the extent to which the family members or friends monopolize the inner circles.)

The other personal community types are **neighbor-based**, in which neighbors have valued places in the inner circles, and the less familiar **professional-based** communities, in which people put their professional helpers (such as therapists or social workers) in their inner circle and friends or family are missing or peripheral.

Does it matter what kinds of personal communities people have? Spencer and Pahl looked at one other important aspect of people's lives: their mental health. During the interview, participants completed a standardized questionnaire assessing a range of indicators such as difficulty concentrating or sleeping, feeling worthless or depressed, and losing interest in everyday activities.

People in two of the 7 types of personal communities were especially likely to have poor mental health. One of the types was the professional-based personal community. Not too surprising.

The other was the partner-based personal community.

People with partner-based personal communities are vulnerable, the authors believe, because "they lack diverse sources of support." If you look to your spouse to be your everything, you have no back-up.

The authors were quick to point out that people with the other types of personal communities sometimes had poor mental health, too, and not everyone in a partner-based personal community had problems. But as a general rule, the person with a partner-based personal community was a fragile and vulnerable spouse.

Here I want to add my two favorite caveats. First, we can't draw causal conclusions from this type of study; it is not experimental (ethically, it can't be) and it is not longitudinal. Second, there are always individual differences. The type of personal community that is best for many persons is not best for every person.

When I wrote Singled Out, the Spencer and Pahl book had not yet been published and I didn't know about partner-based personal communities. I made up my own clunky phrase for partners who were expected to fulfill all of their spouse's hopes and wishes and dreams (and also pick up the laundry): "**S**ex and **E**verything **E**lse **P**artners." In the first draft of the book manuscript, I called them "seepies" for short, but some readers really hated that word so I dropped it.

The point I was trying to make was that Seepie relationships could be great during untroubled times for some people, but they were risky. The personal communities study provides some data in support of that formulation.

There's another more important reason why I wanted to tell you about the fragility of the partner-based personal communities (which single people do not have) and the relative resilience of friend-based personal communities that many single people do have. When I hear from other singles, sometimes in comments posted to this blog and more often in personal communications, there is a theme that comes up all too frequently. Single people feel hurt by their once-single friends who ditch them as soon as they marry or become involved in a serious romantic relationship. I can relate.

I can also tend to my relationships with the people who remain important to me, and pursue my passions, and live happily ever after.

[Originally published at the "Living Single" blog at *Psychology Today* on November 17, 2008.]

11

Is It Healthier to Live with Someone?

Always-single women are healthier than married women, study shows

There are people who believe that getting married transforms sickly single people into healthy couples. I think they are wrong. They use cheater techniques to make their case, and even then, getting married does not always seem to result in better health. Along the way, they spin various tales about why getting married should protect you from bad health.

One of those why-marriage-wins theories is that when you are married, there is someone else around. That person can nag you to eat your vegetables and get off the couch or call 911 if you look like you are having a heart attack. There are lots of ways to poke holes in that fantasy. For example, even if you are married, your spouse is not always right there at your side monitoring you for heart attack symptoms; conversely, single people are not always home alone. Also, it is actually the always-single people who exercise the most.

Even more relevant is a study that addresses the issue directly. The researcher asked two questions: (1) Are divorced, widowed, and always-single people less healthy than currently-married people? (2) If the unmarried people are living with someone (such as parents, other relatives, or friends – grown children were excluded), are they less healthy than currently-married people?

This is not an ideal design for many reasons I've discussed before (e.g., we don't know whether any differences between the groups really are due to marital status or some other way that they differ), but the study was at least based on a good-sized sample. The data were from more than 25,000 white women, ages 18 to 55, who participated in the National Health Interview Study in the U.S. in 1979.

The study also included a variety of measures of the participants' health:

- The participants' ratings of their overall health
- The number of chronic health conditions they experienced
- The number of acute conditions they experienced
- The number of days their activities were restricted during the two weeks prior to the interview
- The number of days in the previous year in which they stayed in bed because of health problems
- The number of doctor visits in the previous year

In studies comparing the currently-married to different categories of unmarried people, the usual result is that if there is any group that looks worse than the currently-married, it is not the people who stayed single. Typically, it is those who got married and then got unmarried who are having a harder time (and sometimes even then, only for the first few years after the divorce or the death of the spouse).

So let's look first at the **divorced women**. In the results that averaged across all divorced women, regardless of whether they were living with another adult (such as a parent, other relative, or friend) or not, they did report worse health than the currently-married on most measures. (On overall health and doctors' visits, they were no different from the currently-married.) As the authors predicted, though, taking living arrangements into account did matter, and in a good way.

The divorced women who were living with another adult had the same health as the currently-married on 5 of the 6 measures. On the sixth, doctor visits, they looked better than the currently-married: They went to the doctor less often.

Now for the **widowed women**. Averaging across all of them (regardless of whether they lived with another adult), they looked mostly the same as the currently-married women except for spending more days in bed because of a disability. When living arrangements were taken into account, again the authors were correct. Widowed women living with another adult had the same health as the currently-married on 5 of the 6 measures. On the sixth, doctor visits, they too now looked healthier.

Of course, the currently-married, the divorced, and the widowed all have something in common – they have had the marriage experience. How healthy were the **women who had always been single**?

Averaging across all of the always-single women, they already had the same good health as the currently-married women on three of the six measures. (Remember that the design is stacked against them; the currently-married group excludes anyone who got married, hated it, and got divorced. There are no such set-asides in the always-single group.) On the other measures, the *always-single women had* **better** *health than the currently-married women*. They rated their overall health as better, they had fewer bed disability days, and fewer doctor visits.

So what happens when we look at the always-single women who are living with another adult? Not much. Just looking at the numbers, it appears that the women who live with another adult may be a shade healthier, but it is not clear if any of the differences are significant. Women who had been single all their lives already were as healthy, or healthier, than women who were currently-married. Having another adult around the house just didn't seem to matter all that much.

Here's a hypothesis I've never seen considered in any of the hundreds of articles about marital status that I've read over the years: Maybe the best situation is the one that is the best fit for the particular individual's profile of preferences, needs, interests, and inclinations. Maybe many people who have always been single like living solo. It suits them. Maybe one of the reasons some people marry is that they do better when they are living with another person, and so after they divorce, they do better if they again find someone to live with. Perhaps for all of us, there are health benefits to finding the living situation that is most compatible with who we really are.

[Originally published at the "Living Single" blog at *Psychology Today* on May 3, 2013.]

12

Death and Marital Status: The Link Is Not What You Think

Staying single and staying alive

Quick - who lives the longest? I'm talking about marital status here. Unless you've read some myth-busting book, you probably think the answer is married people. Some in the Marriage Mafia even push the misleading heuristic, "get married, live longer."

Previously (in this post and in Singled Out), I've made fun of one of the tricks the pro-marriage people use to claim that getting married makes you live longer, and that's to pretend that people who are divorced or widowed never did get married. So if married people seem to live longer than, say, divorced people, they use that as support for their argument that getting married makes you live longer. Some even use that as "evidence" that people shouldn't divorce - even though we can never know whether those people who divorced would have died even sooner if they had stayed together. Another Mafioso trick is to ignore the longest running study (started in 1921) in which the people who stayed single lived just as long as the people who married and stayed married.

When I (or others) report comparisons in which the divorced people have outcomes that are not as good as those of other groups, some people object. They are right that these differences should not be exaggerated. When the data show that the differences are small, or that they decrease over time, I note that. I also note the studies showing advantages of the divorced over other groups. Now I'm going to add another qualification: How do you define who counts as divorced?

I was alerted to this by a study published last year in which the authors set out to look more closely at the link between divorce and death. Participants were followed for about 40 years, from the early 1960s (when they were all older than 35) until the end of that century.

The first way the authors examined the relationship between marital status and death was to separate the participants by their marital status when the study first began - married, divorced/separated, widowed, always-single - and then chart the proportion who were still living over the course of the 40 years. (That's Figure 1A, if you can access the article.)

Here's the first finding I noticed (not highlighted anywhere in the article): When you compare the line showing the proportion of married people who are still alive at each point in time, to the same line for single people, they are so close together that you can't tell them apart. So, **those people (all over age 35) who had always been single at the start of the study lived just as long as the people who started the study married**.

The next comparison looks like the usual bad news for the divorced. The people who were divorced at the start of the study did not live as long as the people in all of the other marital status groups.

Some researchers would, upon discovering that, close their laptops and send their paper off to the journal. Not these authors.

Next, they looked at those people who started the study divorced and stayed divorced throughout. Compared to all of the other people in the study, they still had shorter lives.

Now comes still another comparison. Let's take all of the people who ever got divorced at any point during the study (not just those who were divorced at the very beginning, or those who started out divorced and stayed that way) and compare them to everyone else in the study.

Guess what? There's no difference whatsoever in how long the people in the two groups lived. To quote the authors, "**the mere experience of a marital breakup produced no elevation in mortality risk**." (That's Figure 1C - the two lines are right on top of each other.)

If you wanted to defend the oft-made claim that getting married makes you live longer, could you still do it, based on the results of this study? You'd probably try to make something of the fact that those who started out divorced and stayed that way had shorter lives than married people did. You could suggest that all those years without a spouse must have done them in. (The ones who got divorced later in the study, you might hypothesize, had more total years of marriage, and those extra years of marriage gave them extra years of life.)

The authors actually considered that argument and discarded it. Do you see why? Those who had always been single lived just as long as the married people. And in this study, those who started out widowed lived just as long as the married people, too. The always-single people and the people who started out widowed had just as many spouse-less years as those who started out divorced and stayed that way, but they lived just as long as the married people.

There was no way of explaining definitively (from the data that were collected) why one subset of divorced people (those who were divorced from the beginning and stayed that way) had shorter lives when others who divorced did not. The authors could only offer speculations. The one I found especially intriguing did not even make it into the abstract: The meaning of divorce has changed over time. It was much more stigmatized a half-century ago than it became in successive decades.

Suppose we start studying marital status now, and look at the longevity results 40 years from now. What will we find? Maybe that marital status just doesn't matter.

Oh, one last thing. Did you hear all about this study in the media? Neither did I.

[Originally published at the "Living Single" blog at *Psychology Today* on July 22, 2010.]

13

'Get Married and You'll Live Longer' Is a Myth

Ever-single men outlive divorced and remarried men

Have you been noticing a spike in stories about the secrets of a long life? That's always a popular topic, but it is especially hot right now because of the recent publication of the book, *The Longevity Project*, by Howard S. Friedman (a PT blogger) and Leslie R. Martin.

Longitudinal research (following the same people over time) is becoming increasingly popular, but there is nothing commonplace about studying people for 8 decades! Friedman and Martin burrowed deep into that impressive dataset. By the time they came up for air (and to write their book), they had squished quite a few myths about how to live a long life.

I was particularly pleased to see the 'get married and you'll live longer' myth get pummeled. Here are just a few of the places where you may have read or heard about that:

From USA Today:

> *"Myth No. 5. Get married and you will live longer."*

From Parade magazine:

> *"Myth #1*
> *MARRIAGE GUARANTEES A LONGER LIFE."*

Good Morning America and Nightline link to an excerpt from the book, including this:

> *"Get married and you will live longer. (Myth!)"*

Atlantic magazine (the quote is from Howard Friedman's answers to one of the magazine's questions):

> *"One of our longevity myths is 'Get married, and you will live longer.'*
> *The data tell a different story."*

All of the quotes above are from 2011. Now see if you can identify the date (and for extra credit, the author) of the next excerpt. It originally occurred in the context of critiquing a claim made by two other authors (who also got a lot of attention) that getting married results in a longer life:

> *"They skip over what is probably the longest-running study ever conducted - the Terman Life-Cycle Study. It started in 1921, with 1,528 eleven-year-olds."*

Yeah, I said that in *Singled Out* (on p. 52), originally published in 2006. I wish I could say that my myth-busting in that section changed the conventional wisdom about marriage and longevity, but I think I just put a few dents in it. Maybe now, with all of the attention that *The Longevity Project* is getting, that myth will be down for the count (or at least knocked out for a while).

I have *The Longevity Project*, and of course I went straight to the chapter on getting married and (not) living longer. I think there are ways in which the authors actually understated the ways in which that myth is misleading and wrong.

For example, the authors emphasize that getting married is especially unnecessary to living a long life if you are a woman:

> *"...if you are a single woman with a number of friends and an interesting life, don't think you need to follow the misleading message to get married (or remarried) to improve your health."*

For men, divorce seems to matter more: Men who divorce do not live as long as those who stay single or stay married. Remember, though, that the people in this study were born about a century ago. The implications of divorce may differ over time. A study published in 2009, for instance, points to the possibility that divorce may not matter much at all for people from more recent cohorts.

Here's another example in which the authors could have made an even bolder statement about the problems with the claims about the implications of getting married:

> *"[Previous] studies have found that married people tend to be happier than unmarried people, but this is usually because people who get married tend to be happier several years before marriage; likewise, people who get divorced tend to be less happy before they are married."*

True, but as many *Singled Out* and Living Single readers already know, there is an even more important reason why comparisons of currently-married people to unmarried people results in bogus conclusions: The people who are currently married do not include all of the people who ever got married. The many people who are divorced, for example, are not included. You can't say that "getting married" results in greater happiness or health or anything else if you only include in the "got married" group a fraction of the people who ever did get married.

Here's one last example of something I would have rewritten a bit. It involves just one word that I would have deleted from these two sentences. I know I don't need to tell Living Single readers which one it is:

> *"Emma, forever mature and focused, had chosen to remain single. Nevertheless, her life was quite full."*

Here's hoping the spotlight continues to shine on *The Longevity Project*.

[Originally published at the "Living Single" blog at *Psychology Today* on March 16, 2011, as Maybe this time it will stick: 'Get married and you'll live longer' is a myth.]

14

Suicide: Is It Less about Mental Health Than Integration into Society?

There is no link whatsoever between marital status and suicide for women

In 1897, the French sociologist Emile Durkheim published a theory of suicide that is still being tested to this day. In trying to understand why people might kill themselves, it is easy to jump straight to psychological explanations – for example, perhaps they were suffering from severe psychopathology. Durkheim, though, was a sociologist, not a psychologist, and the factors he deemed significant were societal ones.

One of the most important predictors of whether people will commit suicide, Durkheim thought, was the degree to which they were integrated into society: those who are more integrated will be less likely to kill themselves.

I don't read French, so I'll quote secondary sources. Matt Wray and his colleagues, in the article "The sociology of suicide," describe *integration* in society as:

> *"the sense of social belonging and inclusion, the love, care, and concern that can flow (or not flow) from social ties. Well integrated groups...enjoy stable, durable, and cohesive ties. Individuals in such groups are supported in their lives, particularly during times of personal crises, thereby reducing their vulnerability to suicide."*

Social ties, Durkheim believed, were not just important for the support they provided. They also offer something else that deters suicide: *regulation*, including "monitoring, oversight, and guidance."

If social integration and regulation are important, Durkheim argued, then factors such as religion, social change, and marital status should be among the important determinants of whether people kill themselves. A contemporary sociologist, Augustine Kposowa, explained the significance of marriage in Durkheim's model:

> *"...married life provides a sense of cohesiveness and support that is not available to single, divorced, or widowed persons. Divorce disrupts this cohesion, and accordingly...increases the risk of suicide."*

Single people, in this theory, are susceptible to what Durkheim called "egoistic suicide," which results from low levels of social integration. "Anomic suicide" can be triggered by too little social regulation or "a sudden and unexpected change in a person's social standing, for example, a shift from being married to being divorced or widowed."

Using the data and methods available in the late 1800s, Durkheim claimed support for his predictions. The key question for anyone interested in the link between marital status and suicide is whether the finding that unmarried people kill themselves more than married people holds up to the superior data and analytic methods available in the 21ˢᵗ century. (Of course, the actual link between marital status and suicide could also change over time.)

It is easy to find 21ˢᵗ century claims – both by journalists, and sadly, some social scientists – that marriage protects people from suicide. I described the evidence in more detail elsewhere. The bottom line is this: When the most rigorous statistical analysis is applied to high-quality data, there is no link whatsoever between marital status and suicide among women. Whether they are currently married, divorced, widowed, or have always been single, their suicide risk is about the same. For men, only the divorced have a higher suicide rate than the currently married.

It is not the fact of being unmarried that mattered. Those who had always been single – both the men and the women – were as unlikely as the currently married to kill themselves. It was only those who were once married and then divorced, and then, only the men in that category, whose suicide rates were higher than the currently married.

[Originally published at the "Single at Heart" blog at *PsychCentral* on April 26, 2013.]

15

Is It Better to Have Loved and Lost Than Never to Have Loved at All?

The special strengths of people who have always been single

Even if poetry is not your thing, you probably know by heart the words of Alfred Lord Tennyson:

> *'Tis better to have loved and lost*
> *Than never to have loved at all.*

If you define love narrowly as romantic love, operationalized as marriage (though I surely don't), then Tennyson has been felled by science - the data show that it's just not true. In happiness, health, longevity, and just about everything else that has been studied (except maybe wealth), people who have always been single do better than people who were previously married (divorced or widowed).

As is often the case in marital status comparisons, the differences can be small. But they are quite consistently in the opposite direction than Tennyson would have led us to believe. (I provide a critical overview of the research in the science chapter of Singled Out. Karen Rook and Laura Zettel reviewed studies of physical health here.)

The question is why: Why do people who have always been single do better than people who are divorced or widowed?

Scholars of marriage have a ready response. It even has its own name, with three variations: the "stress" or "crisis" or "loss" hypothesis. People who have always been single have not experienced the same depth of stress (or crisis or loss) as people who have divorced or become widowed.

The explanation has an intuitive appeal, and charts of relevant data often seem consistent. For example, if you look at graphs of people's happiness over time, as they get married and then divorced or widowed, you can see happiness plunging as the year of the divorce approaches, or during the year of the partner's death, and then you can see it slowly start to rebound as the dissolution of the marriage recedes further into the past. (The graphs are on pages 38 and 39 of Singled Out.)

Studies of marital status take a fine-grained view of people who have gotten married. They separate out of that group the people who eventually divorce or become widowed. Then they find that the divorced and widowed people sometimes do worse than the currently-married people. (In other studies, married people are divided by the quality of their marriage, or their economic or class status, or any of a wide array of other variables.) Now consider what happens when people who have always been single are included in studies: This "never-married" group is one big undifferentiated blob. It is as if people who study marriage have an attitude of "they all look alike" when it comes to their views of single people.

My point is hardly earth-shattering but I have rarely seen it acknowledged in the scientific literature: People who have always been single also experience intense stress, acute crises, and devastating losses. If you were to ask single people about such experiences and plot the lifelines of their happiness the same way the lifelines of the once-married are typically plotted, I think you would see something similar. Single people also experience stress and sadness and grief when someone they love dies or when a profoundly important relationship falls apart (and it doesn't have to be a romantic relationship). You can't see it in the results of the published studies because the singles who have experienced great losses are not separated out the way divorced and widowed people are separated from the still-married.

There is something else important about the published literature on marital status. When people who have always been single fare better than some other group (such as the previously married), scholars rarely propose an explanation that assumes that single people may actually have some special skills and strengths.

Think of all the tasks that married people divide between them. The splits are a little less likely to be traditional than they once were (she takes care of the kids and the cooking, he pays the bills and mows the lawn), but they are often apportioned in some way. While the marriage lasts, this can be useful and efficient. When it is over, though, the newly uncoupled individuals are left with mastery of only those tasks that were once in their domain. Even memory is implicated, as when one person in the couple took charge of remembering the birthdays and the other kept track of the times for the oil changes.

People who have always been single, though, are likely to find some way of accomplishing all of the tasks of everyday life. Maybe they master some, tap a network of friends for others, and hire people to do the rest. One way or another, they get things done. I think that's a strength.

Maybe, too, the network is part of the answer. Perhaps people who have always been single maintain a more diversified relationship portfolio than the married people who invest all of their relationship capital into just one person. Maybe single people have friendships that have endured longer than many marriages. Maybe they attend to those friendships consistently, rather than stowing them on the back burner while focusing on The One. Maybe that's why they do better than people who were previously married.

I'm generating hypotheses. They could be wrong. What is important - and, I think, stunning - is that my suggestions are mostly new. Scholarly research on marriage dates back more than half a century. It has been supported by journals, conferences, degree programs, and piles and piles of funding. For all that, there have been hardly any scholars who have been able or willing to step outside the conventional ways of thinking and pursue the kinds of possibilities I'm suggesting here.

My argument is in the spirit of diversity. Just as there were many ways of thinking that never did get much notice when psychological (or medical) research focused mainly on men, or primarily on white people, or overwhelmingly on heterosexuals, so too has the absence of a singles perspective left us intellectually poorer. Fortunately, that is starting to change (here and here).

Finally, going back to the initial question that motivated this post (is it better to have loved and lost...): Of course, my point is not that we should steer clear of love. As I've said before in this space, I think we should embrace big, broad meanings of love. What we should steer clear of are narrow ways of thinking that leave us all locked in small, stifling ideological boxes.

[Originally published at the "Living Single" blog at *Psychology Today* on August 17, 2008.]

16

Why Aren't Married People Any Happier Than Singles? A Nobel-Prize Winner's Answer

Moment to moment, all sorts of experiences affect our happiness

"We draw pleasure and pain from what is happening at the moment, if we attend to it." So says Nobel Prize winner Daniel Kahneman in his recent book, *Thinking, Fast and Slow*.

Some of the research described in *Thinking, Fast and Slow* is based on a "Day Reconstruction Method," in which people relive the experiences of the previous day, and answer questions about their activities during that day. They also name the people they were with during the various activities, and they describe their emotions.

Results showed "no differences in experienced well-being between women who lived with a mate and women who did not." Kahneman believes that the ways in which the two sets of women spend their time explain why neither group was happier than the other:

"Women who have a mate spend less time alone, but also much less time with friends. They spend more time making love, which is wonderful, but also more time doing housework, preparing food, and caring for children, all relatively unpopular activities. And of course, the large amount of time married women spend with their husband is much more pleasant for some than for others. Experienced well-being is on average unaffected by marriage, not because marriage makes no difference to happiness but because it changes some aspects of life for the better and others for the worse."

Kahneman's assumptions about which activities contribute to well-being and which undermine it are based on overall results across all of the participants in his research. So in general, people are less happy when they spend time alone and happier when they are with friends. These conclusions do not address the ways that individuals differ from one another. People who savor their solitude, for example, are more likely to be unhappy when they do *not* have enough time to themselves. Similarly, making love may be wonderful when that's what you want to be doing, with the particular person and in the particular way that you prefer; otherwise, though, not so much.

Thinking, Fast and Slow also includes a discussion of a well-known finding showing that among people who get married and stay married, they become a bit happier around the year of the wedding, then they go back to being about as happy as they were when they were single. (I included the graph and discussed it in detail in Chapter 2 of *Singled Out*.) One interpretation of that finding is that over time, married people adapt to being married. They find it joyful at first, but then it becomes routine.

Kahneman instead suggests that we consider how people answer questions such as "How satisfied are you with your life as a whole?" If you are about to get married, or if you just got married, that will come to mind immediately. The decision to marry, he continues, is typically a voluntary one (at least among the people in the U.S. who participated in the study). Therefore, when they think about their forthcoming or recent wedding, they are thinking happy thoughts. Years later, when they are asked the same question about how satisfied they are with their life as a whole, they may be thinking about lots of other aspects of their life, and not (just) their marriage.

One interesting implication that Kahneman spells out is that even among those people whose forthcoming or recent marriage is salient to them, it won't be salient all the time. In their everyday lives, they will often be focusing on other things, and the fact of being married may not have much to do with their moment-to-moment happiness.

The bottom line in *Thinking, Fast and Slow* is that being married (or living with a mate) is of little significance for people's everyday experiences of well-being. That is especially striking because of something I discussed in detail in *Singled Out* but Kahneman never mentions: When he is discussing people who are married or living with a mate, he is discussing a select group – only those who are currently married or cohabiting. The people who got married (or moved in), had a terrible experience and then got divorced (or moved out), are not in the currently-married group. What if everyone who got married had to stay that way?

Imagine, too, the study that can never be done: Randomly assign people to stay single or get married or get divorced. What would happen to people who are single-at-heart if they got assigned to the marriage condition? I don't think they'd be very happy.

[Originally published at the "Single at Heart" blog at *PsychCentral* on December 28, 2011.]

17

Men and Women Who Have Always Been Single Are Doing Fine

Lifelong singles have strong psychological resources that serve them well

Finally, singles are in the headlines in a positive way! Here are a few of the recent media pronouncements:

> Over 40 and Never Married? New Research Shows You Are Just Fine
> Never Married, Over 40, Well-Adjusted

My email inbox is lighting up with links to these stories. The questions people are asking me are, (1) have I read the study? (yes, I read the original in its entirety), and (2) is it a good study?

Before I answer the second question, let me tell you more about the research. The authors (Jamila Bookwala and Erin Fekete) analyzed data from a nationally-representative sample of Americans, the National Survey of Midlife Development. From the dataset, they selected the 105 heterosexual people who were at least 40 years old, had always been single, and were not cohabiting, and compared them to currently married people who were also at least 40 years old. The always-single and the currently-married participants answered questions about their psychological resources, social resources, and positive and negative feelings. (More on all of those later.)

What's good about the study is that it is based on a nationally representative sample, not just a convenience sample of people the authors know. What's not so good about the study is that it gives the married people an advantage from the beginning. Like the vast majority of other studies that compare people in different marital statuses at one point in time, the married group is comprised NOT of all people who ever got married, but only those who got married and stayed married. The 40-something percent of people who married, hated it, then divorced, are set aside. (In contrast, all of the lifelong singles were included in the single group, whether they wanted to be single or not.) So, as always with all studies like this, if the currently-married group looks better than the always-single group in some way or another, that does NOT mean that if only you get married, you will do better, too.

Even with this advantage given to the married group, the always-single group, in comparison, looks just fine. On some measures, there are no differences at all between the currently-married and the always-single. There are no differences, for example, in the degree to which they feel supported by their friends. (The authors consider that a "social resource." On two other social resource measures, kin support and community integration, the singles score a bit lower, in contrast to the results of other national studies.) There are also no differences in any of the psychological resources. For example, there were no differences in **personal mastery**, which is a can-do attitude - a sense that you can do just about anything you set your mind to. There were also no differences in **self-sufficiency**, which is a matter of wanting to handle things on your own.

The psychological resources of personal mastery and self-sufficiency were more important to the always-single people than to the currently-married. You can see that in the links between having those resources and experiencing positive and negative feelings. (For a discussion of the overall levels of positive and negative feelings, see the note at the end.)

Here's how the psychological resource of **personal mastery** matters more to people who have always been single. For anyone - married or single - the more of a can-do attitude you have, the less you will experience negative feelings. But this is even more true for people who have always been single. In fact, if you look just at the married and single people who are high in personal mastery - that is, they are all especially likely to believe that they can do just about anything they set their minds to - the single people are even less likely to experience negative emotions than the married people are. (But if they are especially low in mastery, they experience more negative emotions.)

The results get even more interesting with regard to the psychological resource of **self-sufficiency**, which is liking to deal with things on your own. For people who have always been single, the more self-sufficient they are, the less likely they are to have negative feelings. But for currently-married people, it is the opposite: The more they like dealing with things on their own, the MORE likely they are to have negative feelings.

My take-away from that is that marriage isn't for everyone, just as living single isn't. I wonder whether those married people who wish they could be handling things on their own, and perhaps feeling more restless and unhappy because of that, would have been happier single. Maybe more productive, too.

[**NOTE** about the overall levels of positive and negative feelings in the two groups: Both groups describe themselves as experiencing relatively high levels of positivity (3 or greater on a 1 to 5 scale, with 5 indicating more positive feelings). They also describe fairly low levels of negativity (below 2 on a 1 to 5 scale, with 5 indicating greater negativity). Specifically, the singles report a shade less positive affect (3.2, compared to 3.4 for the currently married) and a shade more negative affect (1.6 compared to 1.5). Again, these small differences are especially remarkable because ALL of the lifelong single people (and not just those who wanted to be single) were compared to just those people who got married, liked it, and stayed married.

Even those small differences in emotional well-being disappeared once the authors controlled for other factors such as age, gender, education, number of children, and social resources.

Explanatory aside: What does "controlled for" mean? Sometimes two groups differ in some way that is not relevant to what you are interested in. Let's say, for example, that the married group was older than the single group (which they were in this study). Let's also say that the older people are happier than the younger people, which was also true in this study. Well, then the single people are going to look less happy not (necessarily) because they are single, but because they are younger. "Controlling for" a factor such as age is a way of dealing with it statistically, so that your results tell you about what you want to know about - marital status-without being marred by a factor you are not looking at - such as age. It is a matter of showing, for example, that if the married and single people were the same age, they would be the same in happiness.

The results of the study showed that when the currently-married and always-single people were the same in age, education, social resources, and so forth, then the two groups were also just the same in their positive and negative feelings.]

[Originally published at the "Living Single" blog at *Psychology Today* on December 7, 2009.]

18

If You Are Single, Will You Grow Old Alone? Results from 6 Nations

Are singles with no kids isolated and vulnerable in later life?

You know the scare story - if you are single, you will grow old alone. I'll take that scare story and raise it - if you are single and have no children, you will surely grow old alone. Not!

Scholars have been remiss in mostly neglecting the study of adults who have no children, and especially, within that category, adults who have always been single. Within the past few years, though, a wonderful collection of datasets from as many as 9 different countries has begun to be mined. The participating scholars have looked into all sorts of questions about adults with no children. Here, I'd like to tell you what they've learned about the social support networks of older people who have always been single and have no children.

Complete information on social networks could be culled from six of the countries:

- Australia
- Finland
- The Netherlands
- Spain
- The UK
- The US

All of the participants were at least 65 years old. The key question that motivated the authors was whether these older people, who had been single all their lives and had no children, would have the kinds of restrictive social support networks that would leave them vulnerable in their later lives. For each country, the authors compared 12 groups: men without children, women without children, mothers and fathers - and within those groups, people who had always been single or were currently married or were previously married.

Five different kinds of social support networks were identified. The first two are the most limited:

1. *Local self-contained*: people with this type of network are mostly home-centered in their lives, reaching out to neighbors when necessary.
2. *Private restricted*: this very limited support network is typical of married couples who mostly look only to each other for support, only rarely connecting with locals for help.

Less restricted than the first two are:

3. *Local family dependent*: people with these networks have relatives nearby and they rely on them when they need help or support.

In the last two types of social support networks, friends have important roles and other people do, too.

4. *Locally integrated*: people with these networks have kin nearby who are part of their social networks, but friends and neighbors are also important to them.
5. *Wider community focused*: People with these networks have no relatives nearby, though if they do have kin, they stay in touch with them. Their social support networks include friends and members of local voluntary groups.

As you might imagine, with 6 different countries and 12 kinds of marital/parental groups and 5 types of social networks, the results can be complex. Still, amidst all of the details, some telling patterns did emerge. Two of them characterize all of the countries except Australia (which I'll discuss later).

First, adults with no children tended to have the most restricted networks - either local self-contained or private restricted.

Second, there was a big exception to the first conclusion. Women who had always been single and who had no children often had the kinds of support networks in which friends were important - either locally integrated networks (in which local kin and neighbors, as well as friends, were part of the everyday support system) or wider community focused networks (among those who had no relatives nearby).

In Australia, both the men and the women who had always been single were likely to have local self-contained networks. Among the other marital/parental groups, the wider community focused network was much more commonplace than it was in the other countries. The authors speculate that the huge size of the country, together with the low population density, may contribute to different results for Australians, but they don't really know for sure.

So are they vulnerable - those adults in later life who have always been single and have no children? The men in that category are more likely to have restricted networks than men in most other categories. Even for them, though, the vast majority of them (except in Australia) have support networks that are not restricted. Specifically, the **percentages** of always-single men with no children who have local self-contained networks are specified in the first number in the list below. (I'll explain the second later.)

%
59 for Australia (vs. 9)
31 for Finland (vs. 61)
28 for the Netherlands (vs. 36)
 0 for Spain (vs. 18)
17 for the UK (vs. 43)
16 for the US. (vs. 30)

The second number for each nation is the percentage of married men with no children who have private restricted networks. These men mostly rely on their spouse and no one else. That's a kind of vulnerability, too.

For the always-single women with no children, the answer to the question of whether they are growing old alone is a resounding no. They are especially likely to have locally integrated or wider community focused social support networks.

Reference:
Wenger, G. C., Dykstra, P. A., Melkas, T., & Knipscheer, K. C. P. M. (2007). Social embeddedness and late-life parenthood: Community activity, close ties, and support networks. *Journal of Family Issues*, *11*, 1419-1456.

[Originally published at the "Living Single" blog at *Psychology Today* on January 19, 2011.]

19

8 Ways Singles Are More Connected, Caring, and Generous

Why it matters that marriage is such a greedy institution

Yesterday, when I took a break from my work to walk along the glorious edge of the Pacific Ocean, I almost got into a fight. Two women walking behind me on the beach were discussing single people. One of them said, "Well, they don't have anyone to care about but themselves." I thought about punching her out. Instead, I decided to write this post. I hope it gets circulated so widely that it ends up in her inbox.

Here are 8 ways in which single people are more connected, caring, and generous than married people are, and 2 more ways in which they are defying stereotypes and doing just as well:

1. When other people need the kind of caretaking that can go on for months or even more, single people are there. A representative national sample of 9,000 British adults found that more single people than married ones had regularly looked after someone, for at least 3 months, who was sick, disabled, or elderly.
2. Single people are more engaged in the life of the towns and cities where they live than married people are. For example, they participate in more civic groups and public events, they take more art and music classes, and they are more involved in informal social activities.
3. Single people are more likely than married ones to do what it takes to keep siblings together.
4. Single people are more likely to support, visit, advise and contact their parents and siblings than married people are.
5. Single people are more likely to socialize with, encourage, and help their friends and neighbors than married people are.
6. Getting married changes people in ways that make them more insular. In a study that followed people for six years, those who got married had less contact with their parents and spent less time with their friends than they had when they were single. (This cannot be explained as a kid thing. The greater insularity was true of couples with kids as well as those without; it was also true of men and women, and of Whites, African-Americans, and Hispanics.)
7. Single men are more generous than married men. (This is from research in which only men were included.) When men marry, they become no more generous to their relatives, and they become less generous to their friends.
8. Single men contribute more to the workplace in ways that benefit more than just themselves. In the same research that included just men, those who got married participated less often in groups such as farm organizations, unions, or professional societies than they had when they were single.

Here are a few ways in which single people defy our stereotypes; we think they would do worse than married people in these ways, but they don't:

- Single people are just as concerned with guiding the next generation as married people are.
- There is no good evidence that getting married makes people less lonely. None. In fact, in some suggestive research, strikingly low rates of loneliness were found among people we expect, stereotypically, to be the loneliest – older women who have always been single.

Sociologist Naomi Gerstel, who has made some of the most significant myth-busting contributions to the study of single and married people's social ties, published an important article, "Rethinking families and community: The color, class, and centrality of extended family ties." In it, she explained what she means when she says that *marriage is a greedy institution* (short version: "...marriage reduces kinship, community, and even the vibrancy of public life"). She also made the case for why it matters that marriage is so greedy:

> *"Marriage clearly has troublesome implications for the community that are often overlooked. As the population ages, the greediness of marriage deprives more elderly parents – who, ironically, have often pressed their children to marry – of the help and support that they want and need. Marriage can also generate excessive burdens on those who are single, as they are expected to provide the care that their married siblings do not. Although marriage is greedy across race and class, because those with fewer economic resources are more likely to rely on extended kin, this is for them a particularly costly outcome. Thus, not only is the focus on marriage a narrow vision, but it may actually detract from the very resources – rooted outside the nuclear family and marriage – on which Americans depend."*

[Originally published at the "Living Single" blog at *Psychology Today* on October 11, 2014.]

PART III

GETTING IT WRONG

**Dubious Claims about Getting Married and Getting Happier or Healthier –
And the Reporters and Social Scientists Who Perpetrated Them**

20

Every Time You Hear that Getting Married Will Make You Happier, Read This

Researchers won't stop trying to find that getting married makes people happier

In 2011, a group of authors analyzed the results of 18 long-term studies of the implications of getting married for happiness. They wanted to know whether getting married makes people lastingly happier. The answer was no.

I described those findings in detail in Chapter 4, so I'll just offer a brief overview before telling you about how social scientists tried to salvage the case for marriage in a subsequent paper.

Results of 18 Long-Term Studies

In all 18 studies, the researchers began asking people about their well-being (happiness, life satisfaction, or satisfaction with their relationship partner) *before* they got married and continued asking them the same questions for some time afterwards. They found no evidence that getting married results in lasting increases in happiness or life satisfaction or satisfaction with the relationship.

A few things made the results especially striking. First, the design of at least half of the studies (and maybe as many as 16 of the 18) was biased in favor of showing positive implications of getting married. That's because only those who got married and stayed married were included in the research. If you want to know whether getting married will make you happier, you need to look at all of the people who got married, and not just those who got married and stayed married. If you are thinking of marrying, you have no way of knowing for sure if you will end up staying married.

The second remarkable thing about the findings is that there was only one hint, on only one of the three measures, that getting married produced any improvement in well-being. Right around the time of the wedding, people reported somewhat greater life satisfaction. However, that was just a honeymoon effect, and over time, it wore off. Over time, married people ended up no more satisfied with their life than they were when they were single.

With regard to happiness and satisfaction with your partner, there was not even a honeymoon effect. Happiness did not change. On the average, satisfaction with your relationship was actually worse just after the wedding than just before, and it kept going downhill in the subsequent years.

That should have put an end to all the mythology about how getting married makes you happier and more satisfied.

But of course, it didn't. We are so attached to our beliefs in the mythical transformative power of marrying that even scientists won't let them go.

Trying Again to Make the Case for Getting Married and Getting Happier

In the new study (probably one of the original 18, reanalyzed), the authors looked only at life satisfaction and found the same thing as before. In analyses of just those people who got married and stayed married, there was a brief honeymoon effect around the time of the wedding. Then the married people ended up just as satisfied or dissatisfied as they were when they were single.

So how did the authors find a way to make getting married look like a boon to happiness?

First, they looked at normative changes in life satisfaction over the course of the adult years. Setting aside considerations of marital status, the study showed (as have other studies) that life satisfaction decreases over time. Then they looked specifically at the people who stayed single, and found that their life satisfaction showed some decrease over time. From that, they tried to make the argument that if the people who had gotten married and stayed married had instead stayed single, they would have been less happy.

Here are some of the specifics:

- The authors tried to match each person in the got-married-and-stayed-married group to a similar person who had stayed single. Specifically, they tried to find a single person who was as similar as possible in age, sex, education and income. They didn't say when they assessed income. The matching was not totally successful. For example, the single people, on the average, were four years older than those who got married and stayed married.
- At the time of the marriage, those who got married and stayed married reported life satisfaction that was .48 of one point, on a 7-point scale, higher than the matched single people. In the years afterwards, that difference between the married and single people tightened, and those who married and stayed married averaged .28 of one point on a 7-point scale greater life satisfaction than those who stayed single.

Here's what the authors said about their results: "marriage is not associated with increases in long-term happiness, but people who get married are happier in the long run than if they had remained single."

As I described previously, other people – including social scientists who should know better – seem to be using the results as evidence that if you get married, you will become happier.

What's Wrong with Using the Study to Claim that Getting Married Makes You Happier?

There are at least two major problems:

#1

Because the married people included only those who got married and stayed married, it is not fair or accurate to say, on the basis of the study, that "people who get married are happier in the long run than if they had remained single." Married people who get married and then <u>divorce become *less* happy over the course of their marriages</u>. Findings suggest that they are generally *not* happier than people who stay single. (See, for example, pp. 36-37 of <u>*Singled Out*</u>.) On the average, their happiness does not begin to increase again until sometime after the divorce.

#2

The authors are comparing the people who married and stayed married to those who stay single. They are saying that if the stay-married people had never married at all, their happiness would have been the same as that of people who stayed single. (So, over time, lower by less than one-third of one point on a 7-point scale. Remember, this is what we are talking about here: .28 of 1 point on a 7-point scale.) But the stay-married people and the stay-single people are different people. They may have different motivations, different values, different interests. They may be different kinds of people in ways we haven't even thought of yet.

Let me start with the people who stayed single. As I noted previously, Harvard professor and *Stumbling on Happiness* author Dan Gilbert is telling audiences that if they get married, they will get happier. So is Dan Buettner, *Blue Zones* author who recently published his advice in a magazine for the 37 million members of AARP. Neither the AARP story nor the story about Gilbert's talk include any references, but suppose the two Dans were basing their argument on this study.

Consider that some of the single people who stay single are single-at-heart. People who are single-at-heart love their solitude. They are not all that interested in a long-term romantic partner. Among those who have been in relationships that ended, their primary reaction to the break-up was more often relief than sadness or pain. They don't want the same plus-one with them for every social event; sometimes they like to go with friends, sometimes alone, and other times they would prefer to stay home. They like handling challenges mostly on their own.

Do you really think that if such people got married, they would be happier? I sure don't. And nothing in the study I have been describing indicates otherwise.

Now consider those who got married and stayed married. True, they ended up .28 of one point happier than those who stayed single. But they are different people, so we don't know if the fraction of a point difference in happiness had anything to do with marriage. Maybe the kind of people who get married and stay married are people who maintain a certain level of happiness no matter what. Maybe they would have been just as happy if they had stayed single.

Here's another possibility. Maybe for some people, marriage really does matter. Maybe it matters in different ways for different kinds of people. So for some people, they really do become happier if they marry (and don't divorce), and happier than they would have been if they stayed single. For others (perhaps the single-at-heart), they live their happiest lives when single. If they got married, they would end up *less* happy than they would if they had stayed single. For still another group of people, marriage just might not matter at all. They have a certain level of happiness, and getting married or staying single has nothing to do with it. With regard to their happiness or satisfaction, they are who they are.

The important point is that, contrary to what the authors stated in their article (and what media reports repeated and what scholars who should know better also repeated), the study did *not* conclusively demonstrate that "people who get married are happier in the long run than if they had remained single."

To their credit, the authors acknowledged point #2 (above) toward the end of their article: "Of course, those who eventually marry may differ in significant ways from those who do not, and even these analyses with an important control group must be interpreted cautiously." The authors tried to match the stay-married and the stay-single on age, but they were not entirely successful. The singles were older than the married people, and remember that in that sample, the older people were less happy than the younger ones. Even more importantly, the authors did not match the single and married people on other characteristics that could have mattered, such as all the ways in which people who are single-at-heart and stay single probably differ from people who get married and stay married.

Even setting aside the single-at-heart arguments, it simply is not possible to match single and married people so that the only way they differ is in their marital status. Lots of extras come with the official status of being married, that are not a necessary or inherent part of the marital package. American policymakers *chose* to shower married people with more than 1,000 perks and protections that are not afforded to single people. The United States (and many other countries) is still filled with matrimaniacs who glorify marriage and married people, and stigmatize people who are single. What if single people had the same legal and economic advantages that married people do, and were equally respected?

Bottom Line

The combined results of 18 long-term studies showed that getting married did not make people any happier and that satisfaction with the relationship actually decreased over time. The only hint of a benefit was a brief increase in life satisfaction around the time of the wedding, which soon went away. All of these **failures** *to find that getting married makes you happier* came from a set of studies **biased** *in favor of making marriage look better* than it really is.

In a subsequent study that made the bias even stronger by definitively including in the married group only those who got married and stayed married, that group of people (who got married and stayed married) *still* did not report any greater life satisfaction over the long run than they had experienced when they were single.

The authors then tried to argue that "people who get married are happier in the long run than if they had remained single," but for all of the reasons I described above, that is not a compelling argument either. And even with all of the ways in which the study was biased to favor the conclusion that getting married will make you happier, the best they could do was find a difference in happiness of less than a third of a point on a 7-point scale. What would have happened if they included all of the people who ever married in the marriage group? Probably even that small difference would disappear.

In this article, I have focused on the implications of marrying for happiness. The methodological points I am making, though, are equally relevant to studies of getting married and getting healthier, having more or better sex, living longer, and everything else.

All of these unsuccessful attempts to make married people look better should be more than enough to keep other scholars and journalists from jumping off the deep end with their fortune cookie proclamations, "Get married, get happier." But sadly, they aren't. The marriage-addled scientists and writers and pundits just keep on perpetrating the myth that getting married magically transforms sad singles into blissful couples. That's just embarrassing.

[Originally published at the "Single at Heart" blog at *PsychCentral* on March 18, 2013.]

21

They Claimed to Show that Getting Married Makes People Happier – But They Didn't

The parts of the latest research you didn't hear much about

In Chapter 3, I explained why no study has ever shown definitively that getting married causes people to become happier—and no study ever will. Here, I will critique the research (an unpublished working paper by Shawn Grover and John F. Helliwell) that set off the latest round of matrimaniacal claims that we single people would be happier if only we would get married. The claims the authors are making are unapologetically causal: They think their research shows that getting married *causes* people to become happier. It doesn't. The very premise of their claim (that married people are happier, and we just need to figure out if marriage is *causing* married people's greater happiness) is undermined by some of their own findings—not that you would have read much about those results in any of the many media stories gleefully declaring a win for team marriage.

Places Where Married People Are *Not* Happier Than Single People
The authors argue that too many of the studies of the implications of marrying have been conducted in "**w**estern, **e**ducated, **i**ndustrialized, and **r**ich **d**emocracies"—or WEIRD places, for short. They are right that research in places such as North America, Western Europe, Australia, and New Zealand is far more plentiful than research in other parts of the world. But there are relevant data from other places. Between 2005 and 2013, the Gallup World Poll collected life satisfaction ratings from many nations around the world. ("Happiness" studies are very often studies of life satisfaction.) The data are cross-sectional: Married people were compared to not-married people at just one point in time.

Here are five findings I bet you did read much about in any of the barrage of articles or opinion pieces or blog posts about Grover and Helliwell's research: [See the **UPDATE** at the end of this section.]

1. In **Latin America**, *single people* are *more satisfied* with their lives than married people are.
2. In the **Caribbean**, *single people* are *more satisfied* with their lives than married people are.
3. In **Sub-Saharan Africa**, *single people* are *more satisfied* with their lives than married people are.
4. In **Southeast Asia**, *single people* are *just as satisfied* with their lives as married people.
5. In **South Asia**, *single people* are *just as satisfied* with their lives as married people.

All of these findings that belie the conventional wisdom that married people are happier than single people. What is especially telling is that the results come from comparisons that were already biased to advantage married people. The married group, so far as I can tell, includes only those people who are currently married. (I've emailed both authors to confirm this, and I'll update this post if I ever hear back.) That means that the findings are based on the cheater technique, whereby all of the people who got married and hated it are removed from the married group, making it easier to pretend to have shown that getting married makes you happier. But even with that big, unjustifiable advantage given to the married group, they still aren't any happier than the single people (and sometimes significantly less happy) in Latin America, the Caribbean, Sub-Saharan Africa, Southeast Asia, and South Asia.

UPDATE: Shawn Grover got back to me to confirm that in the analyses reported in his paper, and described above, the currently married people were compared to everyone else. He also conducted new and more appropriate analyses in which anyone who ever married is compared to those who stayed single. (Thanks!)

Here are the new results based on the more defensible analyses:

These are the places where **people who stayed single are HAPPIER** (more satisfied with their lives) than people who got married:

1. Central and Eastern Europe
2. Latin America and
3. the Caribbean
4. South Asia
5. Southeast Asia
6. Sub-Saharan Africa

These are the places where **people who stayed single are just as happy** as those who got married:

1. Western Europe (excluding the UK)
2. Commonwealth of Independent States (including Russia)

Think about these results for a while. Look at all of these vasts swaths of the globe where people who stayed single are either happier than people who got married or just as happy. Notice that even Western Europe is among the places on the globe where getting married is linked with no greater life satisfaction than staying single.

Next time some reporter or some social scientist begins an article by saying, of course people who get married are happier, remember these findings.

What About the Research Showing that Any Increase in Happiness After Marrying Is Just a Honeymoon Effect?

If you have followed the research on getting married and getting happier even just casually, you may remember some findings that have gotten a fair amount of attention in the past. They are from a German longitudinal study, analyzed by Lucas and his colleagues, in which the same people were followed for years, as they stayed single or got married or unmarried. Probably the best known findings showed that those people who got married and stayed married (already a select group of all the people who ever got married) did show a brief and modest increase in happiness around the time of the wedding. Then within a year or maybe a few years, they went back to feeling as happy or as unhappy as they were when they were single. So, among people who got married and stayed married (but not those who later divorced), marriage resulted in a short period of feeling a bit happier—basically, a honeymoon effect. It didn't last. (I discussed these results in *Singled Out* and elsewhere.)

Grover and Helliwell used the data from the British Household Panel Study to do the same kinds of analyses on a British sample. When they did the same analyses in the same way that Lucas and his colleagues did, *they found the same thing*: "...the long-term marriage effect for people who have been married at least six years is approximately zero." Translation: By the time people have been married for six years, they are not any happier than they were when they were single.

Yes, this is from the working paper that got all that attention for declaring that getting married makes people happier. You see, the authors did not like the finding that any happiness boost after getting married is short-lived. They believe in marriage and its super powers. So they came up with a way to reanalyze the data to save the day for marriage. (If Lucas had found that marriage was lastingly wonderful, do you think the authors would have challenged the findings?)

Lucas included in his sample anyone who had gotten married and had been in the study for a number of years, even if only one or two of those years had been spent single. His analyses look at how much happier (if at all) people get after they marry, compared to when they were single. Grover and Helliwell argue that it's not fair to include people who have only been in the study and single for a year or two before they married. In that short period of time before marrying, they reason, people are already becoming happier in anticipation of getting married. That anticipatory happiness, they think, is part of the benefit of getting married. If you compare how happy they are later in their marriage to how happy they were just a year or so before they married, then the increase in happiness (if there is one, and after a few years, there's not) is going to be too small.

So the authors did new analyses in which they included in their sample only those people who were single and participating in the study for at least five years before they got married. Once they included only that subset of people, then they found that people who got married and stayed married were happier than they were when they were single, even six years into the marriage.

People who are marriage apologists often like to argue that marriage is more than just the relationship itself. Making that formal, legal commitment matters. It's a piece of paper, and much more. People making this argument are usually saying that cohabitation isn't good enough. Real, legal, official marriage is what's special.

But with their five-years-single stipulation, Grover and Helliwell seem to want to be sure that the people they include in their analyses did not even have marriage in their vision when they first joined the study as single people. Then, once they get close to marrying, they might get happier, but that's anticipatory happiness that belongs with the marriage effect—or at least should not be allowed to dampen the marriage effect (which is the supposed boost in happiness you get by marrying).

You can buy their argument or not. What's clear, though, is that finding evidence to suggest that getting married makes people happier, is not a simple task. Even setting aside all of the methodological challenges I described in ADD CHPT NUM (prob #2), first attempts at demonstrating that marriage causes people to be lastingly happier have not been all that successful. And so researchers persist, trying this and that, including and excluding certain people, until they get results that seem to support their beliefs. You can be impressed if you want. I'm not.

In One Analysis of One Hypothesis with People from One Country, the Authors Did Not Use the Cheater Technique

One of the articles about the Grover and Helliwell research was titled, "Middle age is slightly less terrible when you're married." In addition to arguing that marriage causes people to be happier, Grover and Helliwell want to make the case that marriage is especially good for your well-being during middle age.

Maybe you know from reports of other research (I haven't read it closely myself) that happiness tends to decrease over the early adult years, reaching a low point sometime around the late 40s, then gradually increasing again. It's a "U-shaped" effect. Grover and Helliwell believe that the marriage advantage will be especially strong during that most miserable time of many adults' lives. So if married people are happier than single people in the group being analyzed, then they will be especially happier during middle age. And if, as in places such as Latin America and the Caribbean, it is the single people who are happier than the married people, well then, the single people's advantage will be smallest during middle age. Their evidence is mostly consistent with that, except for in Sub-Saharan Africa.

The authors' first attempt to test the middle-age effect involved data from the UK Annual Population Survey. These data are cross-sectional: They compare people of different marital statuses at one point in time. As I explained in ADD CHPT NUM, these are the kinds of data that just cannot strongly support any causal statement. Initially, the authors compounded their cross-sectional problem by adding on top of it their use of the cheater technique. That's the one where researchers who want to make the case for marriage do so by including in the married group only those people who are currently married, and setting aside all those people who got married, hated it, and got divorced. Then, if and when married people look better, they say, "See, getting married made people happier!" (It didn't. The people who divorced also got married and it didn't make them happier.)

If your big idea is that marriage is especially likely to make people happier during middle age, then the cheater technique becomes even more problematic than usual. By the time people reach middle age, many of them who once married have now divorced. So by middle age, the currently-married group is an even more select group than it was in the earlier adult years.

Now here's the good news. The authors realized this. So they did something I have been urging researchers to do for about two decades: Compare everyone who ever got married to those who stayed single. If you want to talk about the implications of getting married, you need to include in your analyses everyone who ever got married.

When the authors did that more appropriate analysis, they found that the marriage advantage was smaller than it was when they used the cheater technique. But for their one sample (UK), there was still an advantage. For all the reasons I described previously, this result does not demonstrate causality. It does not show that getting married *makes* people happier, but it is a better approximation to a causal argument than arguments based on the cheater technique.

Because it is better in that way, it is worth looking at the results a bit more closely. The authors compared the life satisfaction of ever-married people and always-single people for 14 different age groups, starting with 25 or younger and continuing through 86 and older. On an 11-point scale of life satisfaction (zero through 10), the *biggest* difference in happiness between the two groups was just under 0.4 points. For five of the 14 age groups, the difference favoring the ever-married people was 0.2 points or less. For a sixth group, the oldest group, *the always-single people were happier* than the ever-married people. I don't think these results support a simple fortune cookie type message, "Get married, be happier."

The authors realized the bias in the cheater technique. So why did they not use the more appropriate analyses throughout their research? Maybe because a more defensible way of testing the supposed benefit of getting married would not produce the desired results. In an American longitudinal study of marriage, the researchers conducted analyses that did and did not involve the cheater technique. They looked at happiness and other outcomes, too. They wanted to know if getting married resulted in benefits that remained after the first few years. When they used the appropriate non-cheater technique to look at the outcomes for people who had gotten married or partnered at least four years ago, they found that those who had gotten married were not happier, they were not any less depressed, they were not healthier, and they had no higher self-esteem.

[Originally published at the "Living Single" blog at *Psychology Today* on January 9, 2015, as Getting Married Makes You Happier? No, Part 2.]

22

Married Couples as Best Friends:
Making Up an Explanation for a Claim that Was Already Bogus

To understand friendship and happiness, we can't just study married people

In the past couple of days, the media has gotten all excited about some new research claiming to show that getting married makes people happier. You should always be suspicious of claims like that, as I've explained in Chapters 2 and 3. And, as I've shown in great detail, the particular research getting all the attention has *not* actually shown that getting married makes you happier.

The first thing you need to do if you want to make the case that getting married makes people happier (even though it doesn't) is to show that people who got married are happier than people who stayed single. Then, once you do that, you can go on to try to demonstrate that marriage (and not something else) is what *made* them happier. But the authors' data, when analyzed properly, shows that in Central and Eastern Europe, Latin America, the Caribbean, South Asia, and Southeast Asia, people who stay single are actually happier than those who get married! And in Western Europe (excluding the UK) and the Commonwealth of Independent States (including Russia), people who stay single are just as happy as those who get married.

Here, I want to take on another claim made by the authors, Grover and Helliwell: that the explanation for why marriage makes people happier (even though it doesn't) is that married people (or at least some of them) enjoy the benefits of having a close friend and confidant in their spouse. The *New York Times* said that the findings from the research suggested this advice: "Find a spouse who is also your best friend."

In their paper (which, by the way, is a working paper and not an article published in a peer-reviewed journal), the authors predicted: "those who have a closer friendship with their spouse get more well-being gains from marriage than those who do not." Sometimes when authors say things like that, what they really mean is that they did not get the results that they wanted (results showing that married people are better), so they look for some subset of married people who may be doing especially well, and compare only those people to all single people.

In this instance, if the authors want to show that having a friend and confidant in your spouse is what makes marriage so satisfying (never mind that it often isn't), then *they need to show that the significance of a friend/confidant is **specific** to marriage, or at least that it is even more important in married life than in single life.*

I really thought these authors had finally figured this out. If they had, then I think they would have been the first ones to do so – even though it is a very straightforward and fundamental point about research methodology. (Comparing married people whose spouse is also a confidant to all single people is like comparing a diet plan that also includes exercise to all diet plans, regardless of whether exercise is involved. That's cheating.)

Here's something very promising that the authors said when discussing the importance of friendship at the beginning of their paper:

"If marriage affects well-being through friendship, then we would expect that friendship and marriage could be substitutes and that friendship would be more important for the unmarried than the married, as the married would have much of their friendship needs met through their spouse."

Yes! That's the way to think about it, or at least it is one big, important way to think about it. (I'd also add that we need to consider people's preferences for spending time alone vs. with other people, and how close they are to getting their ideal ratio of solitude to sociability. No one has ever done anything even close to that, though my single-at-heart survey results suggest the potential significance of pursuing that issue.)

Eagerly, I looked for the results of the appropriate analyses. The marriage group would be separated into two subgroups: (1) people who got married and viewed their spouse as their closest friend, and (2) people who got married but who did not point to their spouse as their closest friend. Single people, too, would need to be separated into two groups. Perhaps the friendship group, comparable to the first group of married people, would be those who had a best friend and confidant, or maybe those who lived with someone (not a sexual partner, or not necessarily one) who was their closest friend.

To demonstrate the special value of friendship to marriage, the authors would need to show that any advantage of having your spouse as a best friend was greater than the advantage singles get from having a close friend and confidant (or from living with their closest friend).

The authors did separate the married group (but only those who were currently married) into those who viewed their spouse as their closest friend and those who did not. They found that the spouse-as-best-friend people had greater satisfaction than those who did not regard their spouse as their best friend. They also found the same thing for people who were cohabiting with their romantic partner but not married to that person.

As for single people: They were all lumped together!

So when the authors said that "friendship and marriage could be substitutes and that friendship would be more important for the unmarried than the married," what they really meant by "unmarried" was unmarried couples. Either singles do not qualify as unmarried, or they do not qualify as people. Either way, to these authors, I guess single people are just one big undifferentiated blob.

The authors, again, think they are helping us understand causality. And reporters such as the one at the *Times* were quick to make causal claims, such as telling people that if they want to be happy, they should marry their best friend.

But did that research really show that if you marry your best friend, you will be happier?

As I've explained before (and as anyone knows who has taken even a single course in research methodology, and as the authors should have known), the gold standard for making causal claims is experimental research, in which people are randomly assigned to different conditions. Obviously, no such study could be done to test the idea that the authors are proposing. People can't be assigned at random to be married or to stay single, and they also can't be assigned at random to have a spouse (or anyone else) as a best friend.

So what the authors have shown is this: People who say that their spouse/partner is their best friend are happier than those who do not name their spouse/partner as their best friend. So does that mean that they are happier *because* they have a spouse who is their best friend? Maybe the kinds of people who would *want* their spouse to be their best friend are happier when they have a spouse who really is their best friend. Maybe they are the kinds of people who fall for all the sappy love songs with lyrics such as "You are my everything" and "I just want to be your everything." Maybe the married people who look to someone other than their spouse to be their best friend *like it that way*. Maybe if you could somehow force them to turn their spouse into their best friend, they would be a lot less happy. Maybe they are the kinds of people who don't like to name one person as "The One." Maybe they would prefer to have "the ones."

Maybe some of them would actually be better off single.

Now there's something you haven't heard in any of the zillions of articles about the Grover and Helliwell research that have been littering the media landscape.

[Originally published at the "Single at Heart" blog at *PsychCentral* on January 12, 2015, as Should your spouse be your best friend and do single people count as single?]

23

A Stupid Thing a Happiness Scholar Said about Marriage – Brilliantly Mocked by *Living Single* Readers

Claims about happiness: readers know best

In a previous post, I asked readers this:

In one of the glut of happiness books (Jon Haidt's *Happiness Hypothesis*), there is this claim:

"*A good marriage is one of the life-factors most strongly and consistently associated with happiness.*"

There is a footnote attached to that sentence and it says this:

"*However, it is not clear that married people are, on the average, happier than those who never married, because unhappily married people are the least happy group of all and they pull down the average; see DePaulo and Morris, 2005, for a critique of research on the benefits of marriage.*"

I think the author is trying - hey, he even cites me! - but he still doesn't totally get it. Sure, it is true that the unhappily married people pull down the mean of the married group. But why is that just a small truth that masks a bigger truth, and what is that bigger truth?

That post, only up for a few days, already has 66 reader comments, and oh, do they include some absolutely brilliant and insightful ones - and witty, too! These critiques are so great that all I need to do is add one note of my own, then post a sampling of the readers' insights below.

My addition to the readers' very excellent critiques:

The author is *not* comparing everyone who ever got married to everyone who has always been single. He is only looking at a select group of the people who ever got married - those who are currently married. That sets aside... oh, close to half of the people who ever got married - those who divorced and so are no longer in the author's currently-married group. And then there are those who got married and then became widowed - they are not in the author's currently-married group, either.

So the author starts by excluding from the married group all of those people who got married, did not want to stay married, and got divorced. Do you think marriage made them happy? I guess not, so the author doesn't count them.

So, having already lopped off about half of the people who ever did get married, he now wants to go into the people left in the currently-married group and excise some more. Those darn unhappily marrieds! But now I'm getting to the points that readers made so beautifully that I can't improve on them. So here are a few of those:

#1 A good single life is one of the life-factors most strongly and consistently associated with happiness.
     However, it is not clear that single people are, on the average, happier than those who married, because unhappily single people are a very unhappy group and they pull down the average

#2 A good job is one of the life-factors most strongly and consistently associated with happiness.
     However, it is not clear that employed people are, on the average, happier than those who aren't employed, because unhappily employed people are one of the least happy group of all and they pull down the average

#3 A good pet is one of the life-factors most strongly and consistently associated with happiness.
     However, it is not clear that pet owners are, on the average, happier than those who never became pet owners, because people who are unhappy pet owners are one of the least happy group of all and they pull down the average

#4 A good deck is one of the life-factors most strongly and consistently associated with happiness.
     However, it is not clear that people with decks are, on the average, happier than those who are deck free, because people who are unhappy with their decks are one of the least happy group of all and they pull down the average

#5 A good bicycle is one of the life-factors most strongly and consistently associated with happiness.
     However, it is not clear that people with bicycles are, on the average, happier than those who do not have bicycles, because people who are unhappy with their bicycles are one of the least happy group of all and they pull down the average

6 Having a tree in your yard is one of the life-factors strongly associated with happiness.
     However, some people really don't like having trees in their yard, I don't understand those people. I sure wish I didn't have to include them in my statistics!

#7 A good fire is one of the life-factors most strongly and consistently associated with happiness.
     However, it is not clear that people with fires are, on the average, happier than those who are fire free, because people who are unhappy with their houses burnt down by fires are one of the least happy group of all and they pull down the average

#8 A good drink is one of the life-factors most strongly and consistently associated with happiness.

However, it is not clear that drinkers are, on the average, happier than those who do not drink because people who are unhappy drunks are one of the least happy groups of all and they pull down the average.

#9 In my research I have found that living on a street with street lights is an indicator of happiness*
    *For this analysis I excluded all people who disliked the streetlights on their street. For some reason including those people in the sample made the association between street lights and happiness appear practically meaningless.

[Originally published at the "Living Single" blog at *Psychology Today* on May 8, 2011, as Ferreting out the whole truth behind the half-truth about happiness – oh yes you did!]

24

Genes and Marriage: Their Claims, My Qualms

A new approach to the claim of marital superiority

Anyone who wants to claim that getting married makes people happier or healthier or less depressed or anything else (and there are multitudes of people who want to do so) are up against a hard fact: Causality is impossible to prove. If married and single people differ, we can't know for sure whether they differ because the married people are married, or because married and single people differ in some other important way. (For example, maybe married people have different kinds of personalities, or different access to resources through income or education, and those differences, rather than marriage, account for the ways the two groups differ. The possible ways in which married and single people might differ, other than in their marital status, are endless).

One way social scientists have tried to improve on the study of the implications of getting married is to study the same people over time (longitudinal research) rather than comparing groups of people at one point in time (cross-sectional research). If you follow people as they transition from being single to being married, and find that people who got married are lastingly happier or healthier than they were when they were single, then that's better evidence for the supposed benefits of marrying than the cross-sectional alternative, though it is still not definitive.

Despite the widespread assumption among laypersons and social scientists that getting married results in better happiness, health, and so forth, the results of longitudinal studies are often less than compelling. A recent article proposes a different approach to the causality issue.

What follows is a lengthy critique of the new study of the supposed benefits of getting married. There are five sections:

I. *A Relatively New Approach to the Marriage Question: Behavioral Genetics*
II. *The Study and the Findings*
III. *The Supposed "Marriage Benefit": Two More Reasons Why I Don't Buy It*
IV. *What Does It All Mean? The Ideology of Marriage and Family*
V. *Implications the Authors Draw from their Findings: Let's Have More Government Spending on Promoting Marriage?*

I. A Relatively New Approach to the Marriage Question: Behavioral Genetics

The authors of a recent study (reference is below) took a different approach, involving behavioral genetics. They had access to a nationally representative sample of young American adults that included pairs of siblings who differed in their genetic relatedness. The 1,613 relevant pairs included monozygotic (identical) twins, dizygotic twins, full biological siblings, and half siblings, as well as cousins and genetically unrelated siblings. This allowed them to look at the importance of biological components, "shared environmental components" (for example, what siblings share when they grow up in the same family), and "nonshared environmental components" (what two siblings do not share even if they are identical twins – for example, maybe one marries and the other does not).

With those three components and the appropriate statistical models, the authors can estimate answers to the question of whether getting married really does result in any benefits to health or well-being, or whether any differences between married and single people were likely already present even before anyone got married, or whether there are actually no real differences at all between the groups. As the authors appropriately note, the conclusions are still not definitive. We can't randomly assign people to get married or stay single, so we are looking for other ways to understand the implications of marrying. The authors' idea to take a behavioral genetics approach is a promising one. They also have a great dataset to work with (though limited in important ways).

II. The Study and the Findings

The title of the journal article is "Accounting for the physical and mental health benefits of entry into marriage." In fact, though, as the authors acknowledge, **they never directly compare married people to single people**. Instead, they make two other comparisons: (1) They compare people who are currently married or in a marriage-like relationship (cohabitation) to those who are single; so, this is a coupled vs. single comparison; and (2) they compare married people to cohabiting people.

Those of you who are readers of _Singled Out_ or of this blog have probably already noticed that the coupled people are the _currently_ coupled. I bet you are already raising your red flags.

The authors actually acknowledged what they were up to, in their own way. They admitted that they excluded people who got married and then got divorced. We have seen this before. Social scientists do this unapologetically. Still, it amazes me every time. Let's stop for a moment and consider what is happening:

In a study of the purported benefits of getting married, the authors excluded anyone who got married and then got divorced. So they are going to see whether getting married results in getting healthier or less depressed, but they are going to exclude anyone whose marriage was so unhappy that the couples refused to stay in it.

The authors think they did a good thing, because their alternative to including the divorced people was to mix them in with the people who stayed single. They realized that including the divorced with the always-single could make the single group seem to be doing less well than they really are. But it never seemed to occur to them that if they are going to study the implications of getting married, they need to include everyone who ever got married, and not only those who got married and chose to stay married. As the wonderful Eleanore Wells quipped on a recent radio interview the two of us did with an NPR station, "I doubt they were getting divorced because they couldn't stand all that happiness" (my paraphrase).

The authors looked at 6 ways the marital status groups might differ:

- Physical health (participants rated their overall health)
- Cigarette use
- Antisocial behavior (theft, burglary, selling drugs, writing a bad check, etc.)
- Depressive symptoms
- Thinking seriously about suicide in the past 12 months (yes or no)
- Alcohol use (frequency of drinking, frequency of heaving drinking, etc.)

First, the results of the comparisons between the married people and the cohabiting ones: There was only one way, out of the 6, that the two groups differed that could not be attributed to selection effects (i.e., they already differed even before they got married or started cohabiting). The officially married committed fewer antisocial acts than the cohabiting couples.

Now let's see how the couples (married plus cohabiting) differ or do not differ from the singles, once selection effects are set aside:

- Getting coupled did **not** result in any better physical health.
- Getting coupled did **not** result in any less cigarette smoking.
- Getting coupled did **not** result in any less anti-social behavior.
- Getting coupled did result in fewer depressive symptoms. The difference, though, was small. (For those of you who know statistical jargon, the difference between coupled and single MZ twins was just .13 SDs. The rule of thumb is that .3 is a small effect, so this is smaller than small.) The results of other studies also add important cautions and qualifications; see, for example, here and here and here.
- Getting coupled did result in fewer thoughts about suicide. We're talking about suicidal thoughts, not actual suicides. Check out the discussion of marital status and actual suicides in ADD CHPT NUM.
- Getting married did result in less drinking. Because routine drinking was included along with heavy drinking, we don't know whether singles differed from couples in anything more than social drinking.

So, even after analyzing the data in a way that gave coupled people an unfair advantage (by excluding anyone who got married and then got divorced), this is all the authors could come up with in support of the supposed benefits of entering marriage.

I'm just getting started. There are other ways in which these supposed benefits, which the authors think they have established in a quasi-causal way, deserve even more skepticism.

III. The Supposed "Marriage Benefit": Two More Reasons Why I Don't Buy It
Just a Honeymoon Effect?

Longitudinal studies, following adults as they transition from being single to getting married, sometimes show that getting married has no positive implications at all, or that any initial benefits decrease over time until the married people look the same as they did when they were single. (See, for example, Chapter 4, Marriage and happiness: 18 long-term studies, and the study described in Chapter 5, which showed that between four and six years after marrying or entering a cohabiting relationship, the *coupled people were not any less depressed*, they were *not any happier*, they were *not any healthier*, and they had *no higher self-esteem*. Instead, the couples remained *more withdrawn* from friends and family and neighbors.)

So it matters whether we are talking about marriages/partnerships in their initial years or longer-term unions. The participants in this behavioral genetics study were, on the average, 29 years old. The range was 24 to 34. Between 2001 and 2009, when participants entered the study, the median age at which Americans first married was between 27 and 28 for men, and between 25 and 26 for women. That suggests that on the average, **these marriages were in their first few years**. **Any purported benefits could well be honeymoon effects that will disappear over time**.

What Else Might "Cause" These Differences Other than Marriage?

Using their behavioral genetics approach, the authors have ruled out other explanations, such as selection, for any differences they found between the coupled and single people. What's left is marriage. So if married people look better than single people in any way, it is because marriage "caused" that benefit.

Or is it?

There are alternative explanations. In the United States, marriage comes with more than 1,000 federal benefits and protections. Those freebies are not intrinsic to marriage – American lawmakers decided to add them to the marital package. Sometimes cohabitors in civil unions have access to special benefits and protections, too. Who does not benefit? Single people.

Because of those laws, and for other reasons as well, it costs more to be single than to be married. Maybe when single people are feeling down, they do not have the same access to mental health resources – they can't afford the therapist, and they cannot be added to someone else's health care plan at a reduced rate the way some married people can be added to their spouse's plan.

Then, of course, there is all the singlism – the stereotyping and stigmatizing of single people, and the discrimination against them. How would single people fare if their lives were valued and appreciated as much as married people's are?

Let's consider once again the ways that single people did not differ from coupled people in this research, once red herrings such as selection were set aside. They were no less healthy, and they were no more likely to engage in antisocial behaviors or to smoke. If single people – who tolerate all sorts of singlism, who expenses are much greater than those of married people, and who are left out of the 1,000+ federal benefits that only go to married people – are doing just as well as coupled people in all of these ways, I think they are more than equal. I think they are actually *more resilient* than coupled people.

IV. What Does It All Mean? The Ideology of Marriage and Family

The authors' discussion of what their results mean is particularly telling, I think, with regard to the unacknowledged power of the Ideology of Marriage and Family.

Some of the problems are the typical ones that occur throughout the journal article. The authors have little doubt that marriage is beneficial, and so they repeat claims that actually are not well supported. For example, they believe that marriage protects against loneliness and social isolation. For what the literature on loneliness really does say, check out the chapter on singles in this book. Also, a growing literature on "greedy marriage" shows that it is single people, more so than married ones, who are likely to maintain ties and exchange support with parents, siblings, friends, and neighbors.

When the authors discuss the supposed superiority of marriage over cohabitation (remember, of the six measures, they found one that differed between the two groups), they reprise the popular nagging-wife hypothesis, though without the insensitive wording: "It is also possible that husbands and wives have or assume 'permission' to monitor their partner's behavior more closely, fostering greater engagement in prosocial activities and less engagement in antisocial ones."

There is something I always find interesting about authors who reach for this nagging/monitoring hypothesis to suggest some way in which married people will be better off: They almost never mention the research showing that getting married seems to result in getting fatter.

The authors also add an explanation that I don't think I've seen before: Young adults who marry instead of cohabiting are better at delaying gratification. They take the long-term perspective as they think about having kids and buying houses and so they stay away from all that anti-social behavior. You may know the "delay of gratification" research as the marshmallow studies – some kids can put off eating the one marshmallow right in front of them in exchange for getting two marshmallows if they wait. The cohabitors, if I am interpreting the authors correctly, just can't wait for the two marshmallows like the married people can.

Really, though, the authors do not want to be too hard on the cohabitors. They spend a paragraph describing ways in which the experiences of cohabiting and marriage vary – some relationships are better than others, they acknowledge: "In short, marriages and cohabiting relationships are both heterogeneous…"

If the Ideology of Marriage and Family were not so powerful, I think the authors may have devoted the same kind of attention to the experiences of single life. You know, some experiences are better than others – single people are heterogeneous. But no, there is no discussion of single people or single life whatsoever. Either we singles are all the same or we are not worth thinking about or – my best guess – it truly never occurred to the authors to take single life seriously.

If the authors were to take single life seriously, they might wonder why the single people did just as well as the coupled people on half of the measures. They might wonder how singles manage to do so well in the face of so much singlism and matrimania and all of the marital status discrimination that is written right into the law. Maybe they would think about what is good about single life and what is not so good about married life, instead of considering only what is potentially bad about single life and good about coupled life. (See, for example, *Singled Out*.)

The authors are so sure that getting married is good for health and well-being that they admit they were surprised to find that getting married did not result in any better physical health. They should not have been. As far back as 2005, in that special issue of *Psychological Inquiry* on singles in society and in science, Karen Rook and Laura Zettel wrote a brief review that burst the marriage-makes-you-healthy bubble. Still, the authors are not about to abandon their belief in the health benefits of marriage. Instead, they propose that "the possible physical health benefits of marriage may accrue over the life course." See? They didn't find any benefits but the benefits really are there, just waiting to emerge.

V. Implications the Authors Draw from their Findings: Let's Have More Government Spending on Promoting Marriage?

When the authors get to the part where they spell out the implications of their work, they say this:

"The past decade has witnessed legislation supporting marriage promotion initiatives…Our findings…are critical to the rationale behind such efforts that assume causation, not just correlation."

I guess they are not explicitly saying that, based on their work, the government should spend more money promoting marriage, but they sure are not expressing any caution about the idea. These programs, of dubious effectiveness, are arguably ideologically motivated initiatives that redirect funding away from other programs that really do work in achieving goals such as the reduction of poverty.

Reference: Horn, E. E., Xu, Y., Beam, C. R., Turkheimer, E., & Emery, R. E. (2013). Accounting for the physical and mental health benefits of entry into marriage: A genetically informed study of selection and causation. *Journal of Family Psychology, 27*, 30-41.

[Originally published at the "Living Single" blog at *Psychology Today* on June 23, 2013.]

25

How 20 Million Readers Were Misled about Happiness

Even the cheater technique can't save a famous author's
attempt to show that getting married makes people happier

For well over a decade, I have been scrutinizing studies of the link between getting married and getting happy. With every new published study or review article, it becomes increasingly clear that the conventional wisdom – that getting married means getting happier – is just plain wrong.

The quality of the studies has been improving. Instead of just comparing people of different marital statuses at one point in time, we now have studies that follow people over many years of their adult lives as they get married or get divorced or widowed or stay single. They are asked repeatedly about their happiness (or life satisfaction). A review of 18 such studies (see Chapter 4) showed quite compellingly that people who get married do not get happier.

The more problematic studies (comparing married and unmarried people at one point in time) continue to pile up, and they also fail to make the case that single people are miserable, and by marrying, they become blissful. They could not possibly show that, for methodological reasons.

Even with the usual ways such studies bias the methodology in favor of making married people look better than they really are, singles still look happy. Typically, people who stay single are happier than those who got married and then got divorced or became widowed. I have never, in all of these years, found a study in which the average happiness of the single people was on the unhappy end of the scale.

So Dan Buettner's claim in the February/March 2013 *AARP* magazine just seemed wrong. Buettner, author of *Thrive: Finding Happiness the Blue Zones Way*, was offering advice about how to "give yourself a happiness makeover," and one of his suggestions was to "Find Your Soul Mate." His justification included this claim:

> *"Multiple studies have shown that married people are two times more likely to be happy than nonmarried people."*

I have emailed him repeatedly asking about the research supporting that claim, and never got an answer. I'll assume he is drawing from the same research he mentions in *Thrive* – a study of happiness in nine European nations. Participants chose one of four options to describe their happiness:

- Very happy
- Quite happy
- Not very happy
- Not at all happy

The authors compared the happiness reports of people who were currently in a "stable relationship" (they are not talking friendship or family relationships here – just marriage or its equivalent) to those who were not. Already, that's a problem, because the authors are putting in the married group *not* everyone who ever got married but only those who are currently married. (You can't say that "if you get married, you will get happy" if you only look at the data from those people who got married and stayed married; those who got married and later divorced may have a different story to tell. When/if you are on the cusp of your own marriage, you don't know which group you will end up in.) Plus, the married and the unmarried are different people, so any differences in happiness could be explained by any other way they differ other than in their marital status.

Those are the kinds of problems I've discussed many times before. Here I want to underscore another suspect practice – describing just a fraction of the data from the study in question. That's what Buettner did when he made his claim, but he did not even get that partial reporting right.

I found the sentence from the 9-nation article that Buettner was probably relying on: "People in stable relationships report being very happy about twice as much as singles."

That is a description of the people who checked off just one of the four possible answers. They are the people who chose "very happy" and *not* "quite happy" or "not very happy" or "not at all happy."

Does the twice-as-often statement lead you to believe that the unmarried people were overwhelmingly describing themselves as unhappy? If it does, you have been misled.

Consider the example of Iceland. In that country, the difference between those currently married and all those not married in describing themselves as "very happy" is bigger than it is for any of the other eight countries: 57 percent vs. 22 percent. So how did the other 78 percent of the unmarrieds describe themselves? Most – 72 percent – said they were "quite happy."

Across all nine countries, 84 percent of the non-married people described themselves as happy – either "very happy" or "quite happy." Buettner's claim that married people are two times more likely to be happy than nonmarried people" simply cannot be true. It isn't true. Not even close.

Yet, there the claim appeared, in a magazine with one of the biggest circulations of any (more than 20 million). It was not offered just as a descriptive report (though even as such, it would have been inaccurate) but as prescriptive – find your soul mate, and you will give yourself a happiness makeover.

Here's something significant that did not make it into the AARP story advising 20 million readers to find their soul mate, though Buettner did admit it in *Thrive*: The married people were already happier than those who were not married, even before they married.

Still another thing about that 9-nation study that you will not find Buettner mentioning in the AARP article: Participants also reported their satisfaction with their lives (in addition to describing their happiness). Apparently, marital status did not matter. Even using the cheater technique of comparing just the currently married to all of the unmarried, the married people were not more satisfied with their lives.

The point I am making is not specific to Dan Buettner or even to claims about getting married and getting happier. Whenever someone pretends to tell you what a study found by describing only a cherry-picked fraction of the answers to just one of the questions in the study, beware. If you knew what all of the rest of the results showed, you might come away with a very different impression – a more accurate one.

Another recent example of the bad practice of selective reporting is in Knot Yet, the report issued by the National Marriage Project that has generated lots of discussion of the relative merits of marrying earlier vs. later. (No, the National Marriage Project is not about to take seriously the possibility of living your best life by staying single.) Several key figures in the paper, including ones displaying happiness data, show just 25 percent of the responses. Other commentators have taken those selective displays at face value, never stopping to wonder whether a more complete reporting might have told a different story.

It is no surprise that the National Marriage Project wants us to believe that getting married transforms miserable single people in to blissful couples. But we deserve scientifically-sound, evidence-based conclusions, not just wishful ideology.

[Originally published at the "Single at Heart" blog at *PsychCentral* on April 8, 2013.]

26

The Fraudulent $100,000 Claim about Happiness

A lingering claim is put out of its misery

Suppose you learned from a study that the death of a spouse is a very unhappy experience. The study authors claim that if you compare the happiness of people who are widowed to those who are currently married, the married people are happier. Would you then be able to say that the difference in happiness between currently-married and widowed people can be assumed to be the same as the difference in happiness between currently-married people and single people? Could you say, or imply, that if only the single people would get married, they would gain as much in happiness as the widowed people lost when their spouse died?

Of course not! That's just ludicrous. You'd have to be a dope not to see the flaws in that logic.

Sadly, we have a lot of dopes. Many of them get the thoughts from their tiny little minds recorded in some of the most prestigious publications.

There is a claim that has been floating around for more than a decade – that marriage provides people with the same amount of happiness as would $100,000 a year in income. I have been wondering where it came from ever since David Brooks posed this question:

"Two things happened to Sandra Bullock this month. First, she won an Academy Award for best actress. Then came the news reports claiming that her husband is an adulterous jerk. So the philosophic question of the day is: Would you take that as a deal? Would you exchange a tremendous professional triumph for a severe personal blow?"

What interested me was the claim Brooks made, without citing any source:

"According to another [study], being married produces a psychic gain equivalent to more than $100,000 a year."

I just found the source. I stumbled on it accidentally when I was critiquing the false Wonkblog claim that marriage makes you happier. The Wonkblog contributor (not Ezra Klein) who made that claim posted a link to a study by David Blanchflower and Andrew Ostwald as evidence. That's where the $100,000 meme started.

As I noted in my critique, the authors did not follow the same people over time, and of course, they did not do a real experiment with random assignment (ethically impossible), so they cannot make any claims about causality. But the familiar bad practice of making causal statements (e.g., getting married makes you happy) from correlational data was not the only problem here. The other was equating the magnitude of the feelings associated with the death of a spouse (even if we could make causal claims) with the magnitude of feelings about getting married.

We actually know quite a lot about how happiness changes for the same people over time as they get married and, sometimes, stay married. It doesn't! Seriously. Read all about it here.

Blanchflower and Ostwald had data on income, marital status, and happiness. They found that widowed (and separated) people were less happy than currently-married people. Then they took that difference in happiness and, using their income data, calculated how much income a person would need to get that equivalent in happiness. Here is the precise sentence that set off cascades of wrong-headed claims:

"A lasting marriage is worth $100, 000 per annum (when compared to being widowed or separated."

Based on that, we got David Brooks' claim about marriage providing the psychic gain equivalent to more than $100,000 per year. We got another claim in the *New York Times* that "on average, a single person would need to receive $100,000 annually to be as happy as a married person with the same education, job status, and other characteristics." We got a CNN story with the headline, "What's love worth? Try $100,000." In that article, the question, "How much money would it take to make you as happy as a married couple in love" was answered with: "...a happy marriage is worth $100,000 a year." (Note that CNN is adding even more unwarranted embellishments – now we are talking about happy marriages and about love. The original study looked at current marriages, and did not select marriages based on happiness or love.) We got the Wonkblog nonsense. We got many, many more instances of matrimaniacal credulity. (Just Google some of the key terms.)

Bottom Line. No, getting married will not provide you with the same boost in happiness you might get if you were rewarded with an additional $100,000 a year in income. In fact, the most likely outcome, based on the best of the many available studies, is that you will not become any happier at all.

[Originally published at the "Living Single" blog at *Psychology Today* on March 15, 2014.]

27

Flat-Out False: Media Reports of the Health of Married Couples

Reporters transcribe matrimaniacal claims, don't bother to read the research

Did you see the media headlines this past week proclaiming the superiority of married couples over singles? On Valentine's Day, the Huffington Post featured a story under this heading: "Married couples healthier than single people, study finds." This headline was totally, completely, flat-out false, and it wasn't only the Huffington Post that published something like that.

In the study in question, ONLY married people participated. It is not possible for a study to show that married people are healthier than single people if the only people who participated in the study were married people.

I wanted to read the original study for myself, as I always do whenever I can. So I went to the journal site, but the study had not yet been published. I have access to "online first," whereby some journals will release reports online even before an entire issue is ready to be posted or published. But the study in question was not even available in that online-first format.

In fact, there is just one official description of the study – a press release. I emailed the author and she confirmed that the headlines such as the ones at the Huffington Post were flat-out wrong, and that the study is not yet available. She promised to send me a copy when it is; I don't have it yet. So as for what the study really did say, I cannot report based on my own reading of it. But it did not say what the Huffington Post and other media sources claimed that it did.

The Huffington Post story links to another claim (in the media, not in an academic journal) that marrieds are superior to single people in their health. I have critiqued that, too. Suggestions that if you get married, you will become happier and healthier are rampant. They are all suspect, as I explained in *Singled Out*. It is not possible to test that claim definitively, because experimental methods cannot be used to randomly assign people to get married or stay single or get unmarried. The methods that are used (instead of the ideal but impossible one) are often deeply flawed.

The really sad thing about this latest spate of utterly false headlines – other than the typical egregious singles-bashing that they entail – is that a whole array of so-called journalists published stories without ever reading the original research report they were describing. They just took the press release at face value. That's not an act of journalism – it is just transcribing. Those who went beyond mere retyping of the press release by interviewing the author listed on the press release were not practicing journalism, either, in my opinion – they were giving the author and the university free PR.

The publicity, though, was hardly "free." It was costly to the 100 million single Americans, once again targeted with singlism under the guise of science and journalism. It was costly to every reader who actually wanted to read about actual research findings. Shame on everyone who took part in this charade.

Now, nearly a week later, after who knows how many thousands of people read the original false claim, the headline has been reworded. That's a step in the right direction. But I bet my autographed Mickey Mantle baseball glove that the reporter who wrote the story for the Huffington

Post still has not read the original research report. And the links to the other misleading stories are still there, without qualification.

I'll mention one more example of shoddy journalism about singles, since I have been getting questions about this one, too. At the *Daily Beast*, there is a lengthy story about the increasing number of Americans not having children. In the original version, I was mentioned, but the authors used the word *singlism* incorrectly. I contacted both authors and emailed the *Daily Beast*. One author, Harry Siegel, responded graciously and said he'd get it fixed.

The revised paragraph looks like this:

"Amid this shift, the childless and even the partnerless life has gained something of a cultural cachet, with some suggesting they represent not just a legitimate choice but a superior one. It's a burgeoning movement that's joined cultural tastemakers, academics, neo-Malthusians, greens, feminists, Democratic politicians, urban planners, and big developers. Unlike families, whose members, after all, are often stuck with one another, she praises singles as enjoying "intentional communities" and being more likely "to think about human connectedness in a way that is far-reaching and less predictable.""

Who is the unnamed "she"? Yes, that would be me. My name is no longer in the article, having been deleted along with the incorrect use of singlism (which was rightly deleted – yeah!). So now the "she" is just dangling. I emailed the author who was gracious the first time and I re-contacted the *Daily Beast*, but to no effect. I guess you only get one correction per article.

Maybe I'll write about the substance of that story sometime. Probably, though, you can already anticipate my point of view.

UPDATE: Just got contacted by a Daily Beast editor; the dangling "she" has been corrected. Good to hear.

[Originally published at the "Single at Heart" blog at *PsychCentral* on February 20, 2013.]

28

Serving Up Same Old Myths About Marriage, With a Side of Condescension

Let's pretend marriage makes you healthier

I'm starting to wonder whether it is simply the norm for social science reporters - even in very high profile publications such as the *Washington Post* - not to bother reading the research articles they discuss and even link to in their stories. When I first started studying media accounts of the implications of marrying and found statements that seemed at odds with the published work under discussion, I thought they were the exceptions. Now I think that some of these journalists just call a few people, ask about the results and what they mean, and transcribe the answers.

A recent *Washington Post* story was published under the heading, "Health benefits of falling in love and staying in love." The first section of the story links to a report from the Department of Health and Human Services (HHS). According to the *Post*, the report "found that, in general, married people are happier, live longer, drink less and even have fewer doctor's appointments than unmarried folks." I'm not endorsing the report; it is at times marred by the usual problems in this field that I've discussed so often in *Singled Out*, *Single with Attitude*, and in this Living Single blog. What is striking, though, is that the reporter's account does not even line up with the claims in the HHS report. That report, for example, does not review studies of happiness.

Here's another example. "Loving spouses," we are told by the *Post*, tend to "reinforce healthy behaviors such as exercise…" The actual conclusion from the report, though, is that "marriage leads to reductions in exercise, particularly for men" (p. 6). Also missing is another conclusion that would have ruined the *Post*'s narrative about how marriage makes people healthier: "There is also strong evidence suggesting that both men and women experience modest weight gain during marriage" (p. 6). (In previous posts here, I've described research on exercise and on weight.)

After more than a dozen paragraphs on the supposed magic of marriage and romantic love, the reporter turns to those of us not in romantic wonderland, and offers this dollop of condescension (emphasis is mine):

*"For those who aren't in love right now, **all is not lost**."*

What follows is an acknowledgement of research showing that "strong connections to friends, family, neighbors or colleagues improve the odds of survival by 50 percent." That's great. I'm glad it was included. Also interesting, though, is what wasn't included: The survival rate of people with a broad range of social relationships (compared to those with less diverse relationships) is *greater than* the supposed survival advantage of being married. That's especially noteworthy because the marital status comparison uses the typical cheater technique: All the people who got married, hated it, and got divorced are assigned to the unmarried group, even though they did get married.

Tucked into the last paragraph is a rather hyperbolic statement about the risks of marrying and not staying married:

"Divorce can damage one's physical health so dramatically that the person never recovers. A 2009 study in the Journal of Health and Social Behavior found that divorced or widowed people have 20 percent more chronic health conditions, such as heart disease, diabetes, and cancer, than married people. They also have 23 percent more mobility limitations, such as trouble walking up stairs."

Looking at the research on the implications of divorce more broadly, I don't think the results are so consistently damning. There are even some indications that the implications of divorce may be decreasing in contemporary times. My main point, though, is again about what is missing from that summary paragraph. I read the original research report, and there is a group that does not differ at all from the currently married in terms of the number of chronic health conditions they experience – the people who had always been single. Again, the finding is especially noteworthy because the currently married people were advantaged in that the group excluded people who got married and then got divorced.

Maybe, though, that's why the title of the story was (emphasis, again, is mine): "Health benefits of falling *and staying* in love." It is a step forward to acknowledge that falling in love is itself not enough.

There was one other point in the story that I liked. It was a parenthetical note:

"There are also practical benefits to marriage that can improve one's health but have nothing to do with love. For instance, married people are more likely to have health insurance…"

I wouldn't call that a practical benefit. I'd call it discrimination. Still, I'll consider it another step forward that the matter was mentioned.

[Originally published at the "Living Single" blog at *Psychology Today* on February 8, 2011.]

29

Is Good Marriage Good for Your Health?

Where's the story on what makes for a better single life?

Coming this Sunday to the *New York Times Magazine* (already available online here) is an article by Tara Parker-Pope titled, "Is marriage good for your health?" Compared to so much else that has been written on the topic, Parker-Pope advances the argument in a significant way with this statement:

"The mere fact of being married, it seems, isn't enough to protect your health."

Much of the rest of the article appears to be addressing a more specific question: Is a *good* marriage good for your health?

The question you should ask is the same one I urge students in my research methods classes to pose: Compared to what?

Is a good marriage better than a bad marriage? I don't have any doubts about that, and Parker-Pope describes some ingenious studies of how couples who fight in particularly hostile ways actually have wounds that heal more slowly than couples who are not as nasty. It is not so surprising, though, that a good marriage is better than a bad one.

What about the more interesting question of whether life in a good marriage is better than a comparable single life? Research on marital status is a burgeoning long-standing industry, complete with decades of journals, books, doctoral programs, research funding, conferences, paid spokespersons, and advocacy groups. But the question of whether life in a good marriage is better than a comparable single life is, so far as I know, unanswered.

Simply comparing good marriages to bad ones obviously does not answer the question. But neither do other studies that, on the surface, seem headed to an answer. Suppose, for example, that you are a researcher who believes that marriage is good for you. But when you do your study, you don't find the advantage you were looking for. Well, then you can look at the people who are happily married (or who fight constructively, or who regard their spouse as a confidant, or whatever other criterion you want to choose for skimming the most successfully married people off the top of the group) and see if they look better than single people.

Do you see what's wrong with that? If not, consider this hypothetical study. A cruise line, Royal Pacific, wants to claim that its travelers are happier than those who board a competing line, Cruise Festival. When they first look at the data, though, they find no differences. So now they choose only those Royal Pacific travelers who are happiest with their cruising experience, and compare them to all of the Cruise Festival travelers. Then they air a chirpy ad claiming that happy Royal Pacific vacationers are happier than Cruise Festival vacationers.

That's obviously dopey, right? Yet, of all of the studies that look at a select sub-group of married people, I don't know of any that compare the skimmed-off-the-top marrieds to a comparable group of skimmed-off-the-top single people. (If I've missed any, please let me know.) In fact, you can even find claims made by celebrated scholars, and published in reputable sources, that are just like the hypothetical Royal Pacific boast. For example, E. Mavis Hetherington, in her book on divorce, states, "happily married couples are healthier, happier, wealthier, and sexier than are singles, especially single men." Seriously. That claim got by a co-author, an editor, everyone else at a major publishing house who might have seen it, and any colleagues who may have read it in advance of publication.

What the NY Times Article Still Gets Wrong

Early in the article, Parker-Pope proclaims that in 150 years of research, "scientists have continued to document the 'marriage advantage': the fact that married people, on average, appear to be healthier and happier and live longer than single people." She precedes that statement with a qualifier: "Critics, of course, have rightly cautioned about the risk of conflating correlation with causation. (Better health among the married sometimes simply reflects the fact that healthy people are more likely to get married in the first place.)." Parker-Pope is correct that this is the chink in the marriage-wins armor that researchers are most inclined to acknowledge. But it is not at all the biggest problem with the "currently-married people are better" argument.

If you look only at people who are currently married, you are considering only those people who got married and stayed married. Those who divorce – well over 40% of those who marry – are set aside. Those who got married and hated it get to leave the married group. But when those researchers compare the currently married to, say, the people who have always been single, they do not look only at the 50-some percent who are most satisfied with their single lives.

Still, even put at such a disadvantage, people who have always been single are often quite similar to the currently married. (And, as Parker-Pope does note, they typically fare better than those who got married and then got unmarried.) Yet, even from studies that do find an advantage favoring the currently married, you cannot draw the implication that if you get married, you'll be better off, too. You cannot even draw the more plausible implication that if you get married and stay married, you'll be better off. That's because we cannot simply assume that if all of those people who divorced had stayed married, they'd be just fine. (To be clear, Parker-Pope is not explicitly making such claims about the implications of getting married in this article. That twist of logic, though, is a common one in popular press reporting on marital status studies, as I've documented in *Singled Out*, *Single with Attitude*, and many posts to the *Living Single* blog.)

Now see if you can tell what's wrong with this next claim. (It's not that egregious, so take it as a challenge.) Discussing one particular study, Parker-Pope says:

"people who had divorced or been widowed had worse health problems than men and women who had been single their entire lives. In formerly married individuals, it was as if the marriage advantage had never existed."

See the problem? Parker-Pope is implying that the "marriage advantage" (which is bogus, but I'm making a different point here) has been neutralized. But that's too kind. It's not that the divorced and widowed no longer enjoy a purported advantage – they actually do *worse* than if they had stayed single.

About Specific Studies Described in the NY Times Article (and Some Others) – What They Really Did Show

In that study Parker-Pope mentioned showing that the previously married had worse health than those who had always been single, there were other findings of interest. I reviewed the research in detail in this post. Here are a few highlights:

1. **People who have always been single have no more chronic health conditions than people who are currently married.**
2. **Women who have always been single report health that is just as good as women who got married and stayed married.**
3. **Men who got married were LESS healthy the younger they married.** (This was true even for those who got married and stayed married. What's especially noteworthy about this is that the authors pursued this analysis in their attempt to show that marriage is so good for you, that the more years you spend married, the healthier you will be. Surprise! The opposite was true, even for the most select group of men who got married and stayed married.)

The author Parker-Pope quotes when discussing the research is Linda Waite. Read this to get a sense of why you need to be a bit cautious when listening to her claims and to see how she misstates even her own findings in her journal article.

A few more relevant studies:

- Parker-Pope mentions in passing a study of the link between marital status and dementia. Click here for the details of that delirious Alzheimer's study.
- Want to know about marital status and living longer? Follow this link.
- Want to know how many lifelong singles rate their health as good or excellent? It is **92.6**%. Details are here.
- For other discussions of what the research on various aspects of health (as linked to marital status) really do show, see Chapter 2 of *Singled Out*, the section of *Single with Attitude* called "If marriage were a drug, the FDA would not approve it," and other recent posts to the Living Single blog, such as:
- Is marriage toxic to women? No, misleading reporting is
- Does marriage civilize men?
- Avoid stroke by marrying? A case study in misrepresentation of marriage findings
- Getting married and getting sex (or not)

Final Word

There's more to say about this <u>NY Times Magazine piece</u>, but I'll limit myself (for now) to just one more observation. Have you read the story? Notice how (appropriately) respectful it is of married people – there's no mocking or taunting. Notice, too, the intellectual curiosity of Parker-Pope. She's wondering, what's going on here? How can a style of interacting with a conjugal partner have anything to do with how quickly a welt heals? I like that, too.

But what I want to know is, when are we going to see the same treatment of single people? Where are the singles books with titles parallel to Parker-Pope's *"For Better: The Science of Good Marriage"*? Where are the studies that look closely at single people, trying to figure out how so many of them fare so well? A dating-advice blogger, in trying to make the case that she wasn't prejudiced against single people, said that "being single is way better in a lot of ways than being in a terrible marriage." That's grudging. We need to do better.

I'm not saying that everyone loves living single. But lots of us do. Wouldn't it be nice – and scientifically appropriate – to see an examination of what makes "for better" single life, the same way Parker-Pope looked at married life?

[Originally published at the "Living Single" blog at *Psychology Today* on October 22, 2012.]

30

Great Health of Lifelong Single People Ignored; *Newsweek* Instead Lauds Married People

The latest bogus claims about getting married and getting healthy

A new day has dawned, and with it another study of marriage misrepresented in the media. As always, the inaccuracies are in one direction only - implying that getting married results in better outcomes than it actually does. I've been at this for a while, and I have yet to find a media report that misrepresents findings in a way that makes singles look better than they actually are. (I don't even want that - I want accuracy.)

Here are some of the headlines that WERE published, supposedly as descriptions of the latest study of marriage:

- "Getting married - and staying married - is good for your health" (from Health Behavior News Service)
- "Lasting marriage linked to better health" (from Reuters)
- "Divorce hurts health even after remarriage" (from MSNBC.com)
- "Another reason to stay married" (from Newsweek)

Here are some of the headlines you did NOT see, that actually would be accurate descriptions of the results of the study:

1. **People who have always been single are healthier than the previously married.** (The advantage held for all four measures of health: number of chronic conditions, number of mobility limitations, self-rated health, and depression. Significance tests were not reported.)
2. **People who have always been single have no more chronic health conditions than people who are currently married.** (This is especially noteworthy because this is not a comparison of all people who stayed single with all people who had ever gotten married. Instead, it just compares the ever-single to those who are currently married. Anyone who got married, hated it - maybe even suffered poor health during marriage - and got divorced and stayed that way - is taken out of the married group. Do you see how this makes marriage look better than it really is?)
3. **Women who have always been single report health that is just as good as women who got married and stayed married.** (This comparison uses a married group that is even more selective. Single women - all of them - are compared NOT to all currently married women - a group that would include those who were previously divorced or widowed and got remarried - but just to those who married and stayed married. In the study, the continuously married represent just about 57% of all those who ever did marry. Of course, there is no comparable selection of just a particular subgroup of singles. Yet, even by this rigged comparison, the always-single women [though not the men] do just fine.)

4. **Men who got married were LESS healthy the younger they married.** (This was true even for those who got married and stayed married. What's especially noteworthy about this is that the authors pursued this analysis in their attempt to show that marriage is so good for you, that the more years you spend married, the healthier you will be. Surprise! The opposite was true, even for the most select group of men who got married and stayed married. Among those who married and then got divorced or widowed, the results still were not as the authors expected. Those who got married at a later age - both men and women - reported better overall health and fewer chronic conditions and mobility limitations than those who married at a younger age.)

Now consider this quote, taken directly from the original report: "Those who have married once and remained married are consistently, strongly, and broadly advantaged." Considering results #2 and #3 above, this statement simply cannot be true.

I'm making two points. One, the media got this study wrong. Two, the authors were not entirely accurate either. They report one set of findings in the tables depicting their results, then say something else about those findings when they get to the end of the article and want to sum up their findings. Perhaps it is worth noting that one of the authors is Linda Waite, co-author of "The Case for Marriage," a book with one misleading and inaccurate statement about marriage after another - as I documented in detail in Chapter 2 of Singled Out.

The Basics of the Study

The authors analyzed interview data from a national sample of 8,809 Americans between the ages of 51 and 61. They were interested not just in the participants' current marital status, but their history of staying single or married, or transitioning in or out of marriage. These are all plusses - it is a big study, a representative study, and the authors are looking at the details of marital status history, not just big blobs of current marital-status categories. Moreover, their study included not just one but four measures of health. (The study was longitudinal, but the authors only look at one-point in time, with all the resulting interpretive ambiguities.)

In their sample, some stayed single the entire time (close to 4%). Of those who ever married, about 22% got widowed or divorced and did not remarry (they are the previously married); and about 20% got remarried after their previous marriage ended; the others stayed married.

The authors wanted to show that the previously married would have worse health than the currently married - and they did. They also thought that more marital disruptions would mean worse health, but they found little evidence for that. They also found that those who divorced and then remarried had worse health than those who stayed married, but better health than those who divorced and stayed that way. (What is also evident from Table 3 is that those who stayed single did just as well or better than the remarried with regard to chronic health conditions and mobility limitations, though not the other two measures.)

What the Media Reports Got Wrong

Sadly, *Newsweek*'s report of the study was the most egregious. Their headline was, "Another reason to stay married." Their tease was, "A new study shows that couples who split face health risks."

Reporters Barbara Kantrowitz and Pat Wingert use Governor Mark Sanford (he of Argentine soul-mate infamy) and Jon and Kate Gosselin as examples. The study, they claim, "suggests that the course the Sanfords are pursuing could ultimately work out better" because they are the ones who are trying to stay together.

In the original study, those who got married and chose to stay that way had better health than those who got divorced. What the reporters seem to be implying is that if only all those people who divorced had just stayed married, their health would be better. But that study shows nothing of the sort. Nor does it in any way suggest that the Sanfords will have better health if they stay together and the Gosselins will end up decrepit, depressed, and diseased if they stay split. The only way we could know whether divorce results in worse health than staying married would be to randomly assign people to divorce or to stay married - which of course, we can't do. We can, though, be accurate and honest in reporting and extrapolating from the studies we do conduct.

Think about the people who get to the point of considering divorce. High-profile quips to the contrary, divorce isn't something most people do offhandedly because they can't be bothered to stay together. There might be relentless infidelity, constant arguing and conflict, emotional abuse, maybe even drug or alcohol abuse or violence. It is irresponsible to suggest that if only all the married people would just stay married, they'd be healthier.

Astonishingly, *Newsweek* will not even concede that much. After quoting Waite as saying that the currently widowed, divorced, and separated pretty consistently have worse health than the currently married, the reporters say this: "So does that mean that every troubled marriage should be saved? No one study could ever answer such a broad question." Many psychologists, they add (without naming any), would argue against continuing a marriage involving intense violence or untreated drug or alcohol addiction - that could "make it hard for a couple to repair a bad marriage." (Note the tentativeness. Apparently, it is an open question to the reporters as to whether a spouse who is being severely physically abused would have better health by staying in the marriage than by leaving it.)

The *Newsweek* reporters describe Waite's "Case for Marriage" book as influential (without noting any of the problems with it, as delineated here) and even invoke the debate over whether the government should fund marriage-promotion programs. They concede that such programs are controversial, but again, no one gets a say in this article except Linda Waite.

Let me clarify my position. I'm not arguing for divorce. I'm arguing for accuracy in reporting. I'm also cautioning against the needless stigmatizing of people who make difficult and painful choices, and against the piling up of bogus, stinky, pseudo-scientific arguments in supposed support of the gratuitous stigmatizing claims.

Lessons for Journalists and Cautionary Notes for Consumers of Media Reports About Marriage

Please, journalists, don't just read or reprint the press release. Go to the original report in the scientific journal. Once there, don't just look at the abstract or the discussion section, where the authors put their gloss on what they have found. LOOK AT THE NUMBERS. Think about the arguments the authors are trying to make, and whether the design of the study could ever have produced definitive results relevant to those arguments. When you do your interviews, don't talk only to the study authors. Talk to someone who may have a different point of view, AND who has read the original journal article. Readers, be wary of any media report that does not seem to have met these standards.

Quick Recap of Marriage and Health

Let's see if I can briefly summarize the results of this recent study.

- If you get married and then divorce, you will have worse health than if you never got married in the first place, or if you get married and stayed married.

- If you get married and you are miserable and you don't get divorced - well, we don't know from this study what will happen to your health. That's not tested.
- If you are a woman and you get married and stay married throughout the course of the study, you won't have any better health than if you stayed single. (You will if you're a man.)
- Beyond the study's end: When the interviews were conducted, participants were, at most, 62 years old. Even those who had married just once and stayed that way won't be married forever. Death happens. If it is your spouse who dies, then you will have worse health than the people who are still married. But if it is you who dies first, well - then you're dead!

[Originally published at the "Living Single" blog at *Psychology Today* on July 29, 2009.]

31

USA Today's Big New Story on Marriage Peddles Same Old Fallacies

USA Today features dubious claims about the implications of marrying

USA Today is very excited about marriage. Splashed across the front page of the Health and Behavior section, set off by a colorful illustration, was this pom-pom raising headline: "Federally funded ad campaign holds up value of marriage."

You read that right - federal funds are being used in an ad campaign to promote marriage. The initiative was spearheaded by (surprise!) the Bush administration back in 2005. (The Obama team has not yet made a decision about continuing the funding for the ads.)

Never mind the appropriateness - fiscally or morally - of using federal funds to cheerlead for marriage. That's too easy. I care about the supposed scientific basis for the campaign.

Reporter Sharon Jayson, in one key sentence, perpetrates all the usual myths (and one truth) about the implications of getting married: "Research suggests a bevy of benefits for those who marry, including better health, greater wealth and more happiness for the couple, and improved well-being for children."

Actually, it doesn't, except for the wealth part. That claim is true. As I explained here and here and in Chapter 12 of *Singled Out*, there are 1,136 federal provisions that benefit and protect only those people who are officially married. So yes, getting married typically increases your take, since you get to tap into policies that financially favor married people at the expense of singles.

What are vastly overstated or just plain wrong are the claims that getting married makes you healthier and happier and rescues your children from doom.

In a moment, I'll give you just the Cliff Notes version of what's wrong with this conventional wisdom, because I've already gone into detail on these issues in previous posts:

- Here is a guide to cracking the code of matrimaniacal media claims.
- Here is a recent post debunking the claim that getting married results in a longer life.
- Here and here are posts showing, on the basis of data, that the children of single parents typically do just fine, thank you.

Now for the Cliff Notes. Here are just a few of the pervasive methods and mistakes that result in the perpetuation of the myths that getting married makes you healthier and happier and saves your kids from doom. (Many more are in *Singled Out*.)

- **The cheater method.** Claims that getting married makes people happier or healthier are sometimes based on comparisons between the currently married and the previously married - some of which favor the currently married. But the previously married people DID get married! Using the cheater method, you just pretend that people who are divorced or widowed never did get married.
- **The mistake an intro psych undergrad would not make**. Pretend that if married people look better than single people when they are measured at one point in time, that means that married people did better BECAUSE they got married.

- **The cheat-some-more method**. Include among the married people only those who have happy or healthy marriages; compare them to all single people (regardless of happiness or health).
- **The selective reporting method: Only mention those studies that support your favorite myths**. Have you heard about the studies showing: That single parents are friendlier to their children than married parents? That the children of single parents spend more time with extended family members than the children of married parents? That children of single and married parents in the U.S. do not differ in grades or in the quality of their relationships with siblings and friends? That in some countries, the children of single parents are better readers than the children of married parents? Probably not (unless you are a reader of this blog). That's because the scientific findings that run counter to the stigmatizing of singles and their children do not get much play in the popular press (or in the SmartMarriages) e-mail blasts or in the National Healthy Marriage Resource Center).

(For specific instances of how these methods are used to turn scientific "findings" into marriage-celebratory myths, see Living Single posts such as this and this, as well as many of the chapters in *Singled Out*.)

Predictably, the SmartMarriages listserv was delighted by the *USA Today* story, and equally predictably, they puffed up their piece with under-informed and misinformed claims. Strong marriages, the group declares, help single people because "it takes a lot of strong, stable, healthy marriages to create and sustain a village." Actually, if you base your statements on science (and not pseudoscience or ideology), the opposite may be true. As I explained here, often it takes single people to create a village - they are the ones doing more than their share of the work of maintaining family, community, and intergenerational ties. (That slippery sentence in the "Smart" Marriages e-mail about strong marriages helping single people was followed by a bit of underhanded bashing of the children of single parents. I've already debunked that.)

The *USA Today* story did not play entirely by the Marriage Mafia rules. Jayson included some voices of skeptics:

- Jeffrey Arnett, who provided a wonderful interview about emerging adulthood for Living Single readers, said that the adults he studies take their independent decisions very seriously. About the decision to marry, he adds: "I can't imagine they'd want the advice of a government agency."
- Nicky Grist, the very smart and savvy executive director of the Alternatives to Marriage Project, said that two questions were paramount: "Should government tell people when to get married? And should government and society privilege marriage over all other relationships? Our answer to both of those questions is no."

Let that be the last word.

[Originally published at the "Living Single" blog at *Psychology Today* on February 18, 2009.]

32

Latest Claim: Getting Married Makes You Fatter Because You Are Having So Much Fun

Even when marrying has a bad effect, it will be attributed to something good

Are Living Single readers brilliant or what? Here are just a few of their latest insights.

1. When bad things happen to married people, it's all good.

Let me tell you about a great catch made by Jeanine in a story she saw in the *New York Times* about how getting married makes women fatter.

First, some background. In *Singled Out*, I described a CDC study showing that married people were fatter than single people. The study was based on a nationally representative sample of more than 100,000 Americans. Still, I noted that since it was a study of people at just one point in time, it was unfair to conclude that getting married made people fatter. Maybe, for example, they were already fat when they were single and getting married didn't change anything.

Now along comes a study that actually did follow the same people over time - more than 6,000 Australian women, for 10 years. All of the women gained weight over the 10 years, especially if they had children. But just looking at the women without kids, the ones with a partner gained more weight than the women who were single. [Caveat: The original study is not yet online at the journal's website, so I was not able to read the original article, which is what I always try to do.]

The *Times* reporter asked another scholar (not the study's lead author) why she thought that the married (partnered) women had gained more weight. Before I tell you her answer - which was just a guess - imagine what answer would have been proffered if it were the single women who got fatter. Probably that they are home alone sitting on their couches eating ice cream, in a desperate attempt to sugar-coat that bitter man-less taste in their mouths.

But since it is the coupled women getting fatter - well! It is because of a GOOD thing - their active social lives! They're always going out to restaurants, those married women. (Thanks, Jeanine, for noticing this.)

2. Bad food is perfect for single people.

I have so many boxes of clippings that sometimes I can no longer locate some of my favorite things. For example, somewhere in my collection is a story about convenience desserts (I think you pop them in the microwave) that were described as only moderately tasty, but still ideal for college students and single people. Because really, what is a better predictor of wanting your food to taste great than being married?

I still can't find that, but fortunately (well, not so fortunately), another version of it recently appeared on CNN Money. (Jeanine found that one, too -- thanks again!) This one is about pancake mixture that comes in a can. I guess you shake it up, point the nozzle, and shoot! For $4.99 a can, you, too, can have pancakes. The proud distributor of the spray-pancakes bragged to the reporter about what a terrific convenience food it is, great "for single people and campers."

I hereby invite both the distributor and the reporter to my place. I'll treat them to my homemade buttermilk pancakes with a compote made from fresh farmers-market blueberries.

3. Since Google and Netflix are booming, should you start your own business, too?

Living Single reader "logic001" left a comment to this post that may well be my new favorite way to explain what's wrong with studies comparing currently married people to single people.

My old favorite analogy was to a drug study. Looking only at the people who are currently married, and claiming that they are doing better in some way than people who are unmarried, is a bit like doing a drug study in which you only include in the drug condition the people who liked the drug and stayed on it. You pretend that the many people - maybe even as many as 40-plus % - who started taking the drug and couldn't stand it, should not count against any claims that the drug companies want to make for the effectiveness of the drug. The companies claim that the drug works based only on the people for whom the drug worked. Get it? That's what tons of marital status research is like.

"Logic001" suggested that we can understand what's wrong with comparing the currently married people to the single people by thinking about start-up businesses. Most of them don't work. If you were trying to decide whether to start your own business, "Picking Google and NetFlix as your data set, and ignoring dozens of family restaurants that folded, Pets.com, and so on," would not be too wise. Oh, logic001, you are so right! Thank-you.

[Originally published at the "Living Single" blog at *Psychology Today* on January 12, 2010.]

33

Actual Newspaper Headline: "Married Men Better Men"

A sweeping and dubious claim about married men

Readers have been sending me reports of a study published in December. A few newspaper articles (for example, this one) and this one) appeared under the headline, "Married men better men." Seriously. If you don't see anything wrong with that, consider this: Imagine that you were the editor of a major newspaper. Under what conditions would you allow the publication of a headline such as "White People Better People"? Right - you wouldn't.

Suppose, though, that there was a newly published study suggesting that white people are better than black people. Would that be enough to persuade you, as editor, to go with the headline, "White people better people"? Would it matter what the white people were better at, or would you allow a headline, "White people better people," even if the study was about just one aspect of people? And what about the strength of the findings - would you want the difference to be really big before you would print such a headline? Or again, would you just not print such a headline under any circumstances?

Going back to the actual study of married and single men, the headline of the press release was a bit less sweeping. It said, "Why married men tend to behave better." That's still a broad generalization but at least there's a qualifier ("tend to"). Another version that got a lot of attention was a Reuters report. The headline of that one was, "Married men are nicer, and here's why."

First Glance at the Study and the Results

Lots of people read no more than a press release, or media stories based on that quick summary, so here's some of what you would learn if that's all you read:

- Antisocial behavior was assessed in 289 pairs of male twins (188 were identical twins) when they were 17, 20, 24, and 29 years old. (Most were born between 1973 and 1978.)
- None were married at age 17; by age 29, 59% were married.
- "men with lower levels of antisocial behavior at ages 17 and 20 were more likely to have married by age 29"
- "Once the men were married, rates of antisocial behavior declined even more"

The methodology sounded promising, and I continued to be impressed even after reading the original research report. The authors had access to hundreds of pairs of twins, and followed the same men over time. A twin study, and a longitudinal one at that, is about as good as it gets with regard to figuring out the implications of marital status.

But of course, I still had questions after reading the press release, including one that still wasn't answered after I had read the study:

- What exactly counted as antisocial behavior?
- How big were the differences between the single and the married men?
- What were the results for the divorced men?
- What happens after age 29?

Eventually, of course, I'd want to get to the question of what it all means (apart from what might be claimed about the meaning).

What Do They Mean by "Better" or "Better Behaved"? Here Are the Actual Criteria

So what did count as antisocial behavior? In the original journal article, only a few of the relevant behaviors were mentioned. I wanted to see the whole list, and I found it in this article by Robert Hare. (It is available other places as well.) Here are all 10 criteria:

1. Has never sustained a monogamous relationship for more than one year
2. Unable to sustain consistent work behavior
3. Fails to conform to social norms with respect to lawful behavior
4. Irritable and aggressive
5. Fails to honor financial obligations
6. Fails to plan ahead, or is impulsive
7. Has no regard for the truth
8. Reckless
9. Lacks ability to function as a parent
10. Lacks remorse

You read #1 correctly. If you are a man who is single at heart, and you have not had a monogamous (they mean romantic) relationship that has lasted more than a year (hey, you're single at heart - you LIKE being single - maybe you don't typically pursue romantic relationships), then that alone is considered just as symptomatic of antisocial behavior as having no feelings of remorse. Or no regard for the truth. Or breaking the law. Or being a flake in the workplace. Or having no ability to function as a parent.

I can see how some versions of "has never sustained a monogamous relationship for more than one year" could be problematic. If, for instance, you pledge your undying love and devotion to another person, only to be gone in months, and you do that over and over again, then that could plausibly be consistent with, say, an inability to sustain consistent work behavior. In fact, when psychopathy expert Robert Hare constructed his revised Psychopathy Checklist, he included a criterion of "many short-term marital relationships."

In the study we are considering, though, the criterion is different - "has never sustained a monogamous relationship for more than one year." If you've been contentedly single and have not pursued romantic relationships, that's one strike against you on the antisocial behavior scale.

Still, that's only one item. If the difference between single and married men is a big one, it might not matter. Or maybe the researchers set aside that item in their analyses.

How Big Were the Differences Between the Married Men and the Single Men?

In Table 1, the authors reported the AVERAGE NUMBER OF SYMPTOMS of antisocial behavior according to whether the men were single or married men at age 29. The rows for the earlier ages (17,

20, and 24) show the average number of symptoms for the same men when they were younger. (Remember that at age 17, none of them were married yet, but 59% would be by age 29.)

> Age 17: SINGLE = 1.08, Married = 0.75 (Difference = .33)
> Age 20: SINGLE = 1.48, Married = 1.18 (Difference = .30)
> Age 24: SINGLE = 1.42, Married = 1.04 (Difference = .40)
> Age 29: SINGLE = 1.29, Married = 0.83 (Difference = .46)

These are some of the data the authors present to make their two points: (1) Those men who would stay single through age 29 already showed more antisocial behavior at age 17 than those who would marry, even though at age 17 no one was married yet. (2) Once married, the difference in antisocial behavior between singles and marrieds is even greater.

All of that is true. But look at the actual numbers! The biggest number of symptoms for any group at any age is 1.48. Now most of those antisocial behaviors are pretty bad behaviors, so having one or two of them (depending on what they are) may be no small thing. But now look at the numbers that are even more important - the DIFFERENCES in the number of antisocial behaviors between the married and the single men. Every difference is an average of less than half a symptom.

So these are the findings behind the headlines, "Married men better men." At age 29, single men report just over 1 anti-social behavior, and married men report just under 1 anti-social behavior. As far as I can tell, that one behavior could include "has never sustained a monogamous relationship for more than one year." If the authors set that item aside, they didn't say so.

Engaging in just 1 anti-social behavior does not mean that you have antisocial personality disorder. For that, you would have to engage in at least 3 of them (plus meet some other criteria). So how many of the men in the study engaged in 3 or more of the antisocial behaviors? The authors told us: 3.9%. They also estimated that marriage resulted in a 30% reduction in antisocial behaviors. All of this is tentative and qualified but let's go with it to get a hint about the actual differences between the single and the married men. Solving the equations, I come up with 13 single men with antisocial behavior disorder and 9 married men. That's a difference of 4 men (out of 289 singles and 289 marrieds). That, too, gives you a sense of what is behind the headlines claiming that married men are better men.

What Were the Results for the Divorced Men? What Happened After Age 29?
The results for the divorced men matter because in studies of other implications of marital status, such as health or happiness, divorced people sometimes fare worse than people who have always been single. When that happens, then the risk is not staying single, it is getting married and then unmarried. You can't say that getting married makes your life better if that's only true for people who get married and stay married.

There were only 18 divorced men out of the 289 twin pairs, and the authors coded them as single, rather than analyzing them separately. They also tried leaving them out entirely, and said it made no difference. The divorced men would be worth revisiting in future years, when there are likely to be more of them. The relevant question is: Does the rate of antisocial behavior change when men transition from being married to being divorced, and how does that rate compare to that of the men who stayed single?

We don't know what happens after age 29, because the data collection (as reported in this study) ended at that age. That's important, though. As the authors note, "antisocial behavior is more common in early adulthood." So the highest rate the authors found for either of the groups at any of the ages was 1.48 behaviors. The biggest difference between married and single men was 0.46 behaviors. Looking past age 29, the overall rate is likely to decrease. Perhaps the difference will, too.

In my next post (the next article in this book), I'll address the questions of what these study results really mean, and who is really nicer, married men or single men.

[Originally published at the "Living Single" blog at *Psychology Today* on January 8, 2011.]

34

Naughty or Nice? Single Men and Married Men

Deciding what counts as naughty or nice

In my previous post, I took on headlines claiming that married men are better men (or at least better behaved, or nicer, or less likely to be psychopaths) in my favorite way - by looking at the original journal article to see what the results really were. Take a look at the details if you haven't already; the short version is that saying "married men are better men" is at best a stretch; in fact, if we had more information, it is possible that we would conclude that the results suggest something entirely different.

What Do the Study Results Really Mean?

First, let me reiterate that we don't know whether there would be any difference at all between the antisocial behaviors of married and single men if the item about a 1-year monogamous relationship were set aside. It is even possible that the married men would average more antisocial behaviors than the single men (since the average difference between the two groups was less than half of one behavior).

What if the results were the same even if that one item were set aside? Why would the men who average just over 1 antisocial behavior at age 17 be more likely to stay single than those who average just under 1 antisocial behavior? And why would the difference in antisocial behaviors become even greater by the time 59% of the men had married, at age 29? (Again, by a "greater" difference, we mean that the 17-year olds who would stay single averaged 0.33 more antisocial behaviors than those who would marry; by 29, the difference would be 0.46 antisocial behaviors.)

The authors speculate that the (slightly) more antisocial men are less likely to marry because they are less attractive as marriage partners or they find marriage less attractive themselves. More interesting were the speculations as to why marriage seems to be associated with a decrease in antisocial behaviors. From the press release:

"...it's unlikely that marriage inhibits men's antisocial behavior directly, but rather than marriage is a marker for other factors such as social bonding or less time spent with delinquent peers. Another factor that seems to be important is marriage quality..."

From reading the original research report, I know what they mean by "social bonding" - cohabiting or being engaged, rather than just being married. They do NOT seem to be saying that having important people in your life is what matters - instead they are saying that having a romantic partner is what matters. They are also setting up a good vs. bad contrast: romantic partner = good; friends = bad, delinquent. It is true that friends can egg one another into bad behaviors but they can also be a powerful force for good. (Remember who provided the most difficult and emotionally wrenching help during the height of the AIDS crisis?) The evidence for the potential benefits of friendship, even during ordinary times, is growing.

The qualifier about marriage quality is significant, too. The research article about antisocial behavior begins with the proclamation that "there is now convincing evidence that the state of marriage is associated with lower crime rates." I looked at the papers cited in support of that, and recognized one that I had already critiqued in *Singled Out*. Here's what I said about it:

> *"Did the delinquent boys who married become less lawless? Actually, they did, gradually. But only if their marriages were good ones, meaning that their relationship 'evolves into a strong attachment.' The delinquents whose marriages were not as good often got into even more trouble than they had when they were bachelors."*

So Who Is Really 'Nicer' or 'Better," Single Men Or Married Men?

Seems to me that if you are going to print a broad, damning headline, indicating that married men are "better" or "nicer" than single men, you had better be referring to something more than one type of behavior that (happily) occurs at a very low rate in the population, and that separates married and single men by less than one "symptom."

That, of course, would mean looking at a much wider range of ways that getting married may or may not matter in the lives of men. In a previous post and in *Singled Out*, I looked closely at the results of a study of marriage in men's lives. The study included an assessment of how often married and single men gave gifts of more than $200. Here's the short version of the answer:

"In sum, men who are single give no less to relatives than men who are married, despite drawing from one (rather than two) incomes and getting paid less to boot. And, they give more to friends than married men do."

How does that square with married men being "nicer"?

What about devoting time to service-oriented groups or organizations? Here's another excerpt from the same sources:

"One of the cliches about marriage is that it takes self-centered singles and turns them into concerned citizens. By marrying, the story goes, adults begin to feel that they have a stake in the fate of the nation that they did not have as self-absorbed singles. If this were true, then married people might be expected to put their time where their values are. They may, for example, devote more time to just those organizations billed as providing service to the community and to society. They might also become more involved in political groups. Nock looked into these possibilities, too. But he found no differences. Men who married spent no more time in service clubs, political groups, or fraternal organizations than they had when they were single." They actually spent less time in groups such as professional societies, unions, and farm organizations.

Check out this post, too, "Does marriage civilize men," for more examples of the debunking of false claims about the transformative power of marriage in men's lives.

UPDATE: Here's a New York Times column on the study, by Pamela Paul, that includes part of my point.

[Originally published at the "Living Single" blog at *Psychology Today* on January 11, 2011.]

35

Will Marriage Save You from Dying of Cancer?

The latest study is hardly definitive

When I was out of the country a few weeks ago, the latest study proclaiming that single people are doomed followed me around. It was in the headlines of newspapers in the airports, and a story about it in another language was shown to me by a journalist at a conference where I was speaking – about the stereotyping and stigmatizing of single people that I call singlism. Ironic, in a way.

I'm talking about the study of marital status and cancer, claiming, predictably, that married cancer patients fare better than single ones: they are more likely to get diagnosed before the cancer has spread, they are more likely to receive the treatment considered definitive, and they are more likely to survive their cancer. (I already started writing about this study elsewhere); because it has gotten so much attention, I want to give as much attention as I can to a critique, so I'm writing about it here, too.)

The researchers compared patients who were currently married to those who were not married (divorced or widowed or always-single). That last sentence right there tells you something essential about the research. *This is a study from which definitive causal conclusions can **never** be drawn.* No matter how many stories you may have read about this research suggesting that the married patients did better *because* they were married, none of them had any sound scientific basis for making that claim.

Most of the stories I read did not just proclaim that "married cancer patients live longer" (that exact headline is from the *New York Times* – I'll critique their story in detail later); they went on to tell us why that happened. Most explanations pointed to social support and nagging (though they did not use that N word) – married patients have a spouse to make sure they get to the doctor quickly and who support them as they deal with the disease; single people, the hackneyed story goes, don't have anyone.

Now here's something that none of the media reports mentioned: All of the suggested explanations were just guesses. Social support was not measured. Nagging was not measured.

If you want to know more of the details of the study, read the next section. Otherwise, skip to the following section where I resume making fun of all of the bad reporting about it in the media, and most embarrassingly, in an editorial that appeared in the journal that published the original research (*Journal of Clinical Oncology*). The authors actually did include some of the most important caveats in their article, but what fun would it be for the media to admit that marriage may have had nothing to do with the findings?

The Details of the Research

(The original article may be either unavailable in its entirely or behind a pay wall. If you cannot access it, the best summary I found is this one from the U.S. National Library of Medicine, which spells out the most compelling alternative explanation to the one you heard so often in the media.)

The National Cancer Institute maintains a huge database of information on the incidence, treatment, and survival from cancer. The researchers examined data from more than 700,000 people 18 and older who had been diagnosed between 2004 and 2008 with one of the 10 deadliest cancers.

Controlling for age, sex, race, education, household income, and rural vs. urban residence, the researchers found that unmarried patients who were first diagnosed were more likely to have a cancer that had spread than were the currently married patients.

Next, they looked only at those 500,000+ patients whose cancer had not spread. They determined whether the patients had gotten the treatment (either surgery and/or radiation – no information on chemotherapy was available) considered definitive for their type of cancer. They found that after adjusting for the demographic factors as well as the tumor and nodal stage, the married patients "were more likely to undergo definitive surgical and/or radiotherapeutic management" than the unmarried patients. (The authors suggested that "the most likely reason is that married patients have better adherence with prescribed treatments than unmarried patients.")

Finally, survival rates were analyzed as of about 3 years after the diagnosis. Married patients were less likely to have died from their cancer than were the unmarried patients.

The currently married patients also fared better than the unmarried patients when they were compared to each category of unmarried people (divorced, widowed, always-single) and not just when all of those subgroups were combined.

Finally, all three of the supposed advantages of marriage were greater for the men than for the women.

Did You Notice the Problems that All of the Media Stories – and the Editorial in the Medical Journal – Missed?

The story being told about the findings of this study is that married people with cancer fared better than unmarried people because they were married, and marriage comes with benefits such as social support and encouragement to get to the doctor sooner.

The key question is: What other explanation is possible? Is there a different reason why married people might seem to fare better in the ways measured in this study?

Here's another hint. To claim that cancer patients do better because they are married is to say that if single people would get married, they would do better, too. Another implication of that claim is that if only the divorced people had stayed married, they too would be more likely to survive cancer. Do you buy that? If not, what does that tell you about how to think about the results?

A Few Alternative Ways of Explaining the Study

#1 Married people have more money

There is plenty of evidence that married people are economically advantaged over single people. They have the benefit of financial favoritism built right into federal laws. (That's one of the reasons motivating the advocacy of official, legal same-sex marriage.) Single people are also targets of economic discrimination. For example, single men are paid less than married men even when they have been on the job the same number of years with the same level of accomplishments, and even when they are twins.

The authors did take household income into consideration but economic assets include more than just income. The greater wealth of married people could account for their getting to the doctor sooner, getting the best available treatment, and being more likely to survive their cancer.

#2 *Married people have more access to health care*

With more money comes more options for high quality health care – or any health care at all. Even apart from differences in wealth, though, there are differences in access to health insurance. For example, married people sometimes have access to health insurance through their spouse's plan. Single people do not.

If single people had as much money and as much access to health insurance as married people, maybe they would fare just as well as married people when struck by cancer.

#3 *Doctors and nurses discriminate against single patients*

In *Singled Out*, I reviewed research on discrimination against single people by medical professionals. In a particularly telling study, physicians admitted that they provided better care and more complete care to patients who had supportive families than to those who seemed to be alone. What's more, they said that other doctors, nurses, and staff also did the same.

If doctors provide better quality care to their married patients than to their single patients, then perhaps it should come as no surprise if married people show up at their doctors' doorsteps sooner, if they are more likely to get the definitive treatment, and if they are more likely to survive their cancers.

More evidence for this explanation comes from a series of studies just published a few months ago in Sweden. In a study of patients with newly metastasized cancer, those who were living alone were prescribed less combination chemotherapy and surgery than patients who were not living alone. In another study in which Swedish oncologists were interviewed, the doctors said that they worried that patients living alone did not have social support, and so they ordered less chemo for them.

#4 *Married people and single people are different people – any way that they differ, other than in marital status, could explain differences in health outcomes*

The authors found that in their dataset, the married patients were younger than the unmarried patients and they had higher incomes and more education. They controlled for those factors statistically, so perhaps those particular factors do not explain the results, but any other differences between the two groups might.

Consider, for example, that some of the unmarried patients may have been single-at-heart. They are people who live their best and most meaningful lives as single people. They do not want to be married. If people who are single-at-heart were badgered into getting married (perhaps in part by media stories telling them that if they stay single, they will die of cancer), do you really think they would be healthier?

Or say you are married and miserable. You want to get divorced but now you wonder whether transitioning into an unmarried state will kill you. Seriously?

There's another difference between always-single people and married people that has long intrigued me. Single people value meaningful work more than married people do. It is a difference that shows up even in prospective studies in which people are first asked about their values in high school. Those who will stay single already value meaningful work more than those who will marry.

If single people value quality of work more than married people do, then maybe on the average, they value quality of life more, too. Suppose you knew that if you went to the doctor more often, and – if diagnosed with cancer – you submitted to every version of slashing and burning and poisoning that anyone recommended, you would live a few years longer? Now suppose your choice was to skip all that and live your life as fully and freely as possible, outside of hospitals and doctors' offices? I have never been faced with that choice, but I think I would be very tempted to choose the latter. That's not an indication of valuing life less but of valuing quality of life more. For cancers that are especially deadly, such as the pancreatic cancer that runs in my family, the odds that any treatment will be successful are slim.

Now about All that Social Support that Married People Supposedly Get

The belief that married people are interpersonally connected and socially supported, whereas single people are isolated and "don't have anyone," is a myth. It is a stereotype that has been debunked by a variety of studies with a variety of research designs. (Here are some of them.)

There is also some evidence to suggest that a husband may not be such a great source of support for women with cancer, and that friends may well be. Studies of women with breast cancer have shown that husbands are, on the average, not very good at relieving women's stress or helping them recover more quickly (Bolger et al., 1996). But if those women have supportive friends, then it did not matter if their husbands were not supportive – they could still cope reasonably well with the help of their friends (Manne et al., 2003).

Remember, too, that in the study in question, no supportive behaviors were monitored or measured, and neither were any coping behaviors. We really don't know if the married people got more support than the single people did, whether they complied with the recommended medical regimen more, or anything else.

[Originally published at the "Living Single" blog at *Psychology Today* on October 21, 2013.]

36

Singles Doomed to Early Grave – Not by Their Single Lives But by the Cheater Technique

Set aside the marrieds who hated marriage, then marriage wins!

Ready yourselves, single people! A just-published article claims that people who stay single are headed straight to the grave - and fast. Faster than people who are currently married. The media is already on it, as with today's MSNBC headline, "Single people may die younger, new study finds."

If you are a regular reader of Living Single, or if you read *Singled Out* or *Single with Attitude*, you will recognize something in that very first paragraph that tells you all you need to know about why this latest scare story is bogus. See what it is?

A vast academic literature is often drawn upon to make one simple proclamation - Married People Win! The claim is based on the typical cheater technique in which a group comprised of everyone who stays single - whether they want to be single or not - is compared to the group of people currently married. So the comparison group is not all of the people who ever got married. That's the appropriate group to use if you want somewhat respectable scientific grounds for saying to single people that if they get married, they will live longer. No, that's not the comparison group. Instead, all of the people who got married, hated it, and then divorced (and all of the people who got married and became widowed) are removed from the comparison group. That's not good science - it's a set-up.

If it is still yet clear what's wrong with that sort of comparison (all people who stay single vs. only those people who got married and are still married), I'll give you the short version here. The more detailed explanations are in Chapter 2 of *Singled Out* and the section of *Single with Attitude* called, "If Marriage Were a Drug, the FDA Would Not Approve It." There is also a less detailed version in this post.

I typically use the example of the hypothetical new drug, Shamster, but it's summer, so I'll try a cruise line variation. Festival Cruise Lines is in competition with Royal Treatment Cruises. Festival has access to satisfaction ratings from all of the people who ever cruised on either line. Some people tried Festival, hated it, and never cruised with them again. Maybe they, along with most of the other people onboard, got sick. Maybe the service was lousy or the food was disappointing or the rooms were tiny. Whatever. So Festival decides to include in their analyses only those people who rated their Festival experiences positively and continue to book cruises with Festival. They compare those satisfaction ratings with the ratings of everyone who ever cruised on Royal Treatment, whether they liked their experiences or not. What's more, the number of people who hated their Festival experiences was close to 50%! Knowing all that, what would you make of the claim that people who currently cruise with Festival are happier cruisers than Royal Treatment customers? Would you assume that you should cruise with Festival, too? I didn't think so.

Don't expect social scientists to get all apologetic about the bogus comparison. It's their standard practice, and has been for as long as this sort of research has been conducted. Their defense might be that they are clear about who is in each group - all people who stayed single vs. those who are currently married. Their claim is that people who are currently married are happier (or live longer, or whatever today's bogus story may be) than those who are single and always have been. Technically true, perhaps. But again, what would you make of the comparable claim that the current customers of

Festival are happier than all of the customers of Royal Treatment? (I know, my <u>drug example</u> works better, but I just wanted to do something different for once.)

In scientific papers, there is almost always a section in which the authors are made to fess up about the limitations of their study. If the authors recognized the cheater technique I have described so often, or if they were willing to admit it, you would find that concession in the limitations section. It is not in the review paper on mortality that I'm discussing, and it is hardly ever in any other paper. That concession would not sit well with the ruling narrative that Married People Win.

It is interesting in a way, because there are two popular "explanations" for the bogus claim that Married People Win that should nudge at least some social scientists into realizing what's wrong with their comparison. Those explanations are "selection" and "protection." The selection argument says that you can't compare currently married people to single people at one point in time and say that marriage made people happier, because perhaps the married people were happier (or healthier or whatever) than the single people even before they married. The protection explanation says that married people win because their spouse protects them from unhappiness, ill health, an early demise, or any other bad outcome. The fact that those same social scientists don't realize that there is also selection *out of* marriage (divorce, widowhood), and that selection *out* could potentially be even more important than selection *in*, continues to astound me.

Some Details of the Meta-Analysis

The article on mortality is a meta-analysis, which is a quantitative summary of all of the available studies on a particular topic. The article reports on 90 studies for the most relevant analyses, and the total number of people who participated in those 90 studies was about 500 million. Sounds impressive, doesn't it? I'll come back to that in the "Bottom Line" section, below.

The studies that were included compared mortality from all causes for currently married people and people who had always been single. Studies of death from just one cause or set of causes (e.g., heart disease) were excluded. Each study includes a baseline age - the age of the participants when the study started. So if you started a study of 40-year olds right now, the baseline age would be 40 and the baseline year would be 2011. (You don't need to pick just one age.) You would find out who was currently married and who had always been single, then sometime in the future (say, 10 years later, but it can be any number, or you can follow them repeatedly), you see who's still standing.

The results are presented in what are called "hazard ratios." (Appropriate enough - it is hazardous to die.) They are relative risks of dying for the two groups. If the ratio is 1, then currently-married and always-single people have the same risk of dying within the time period of the study. The data were coded so that numbers greater than 1 meant that more of the always-single people died. The average result across all of the studies was 1.30, meaning that the always-singles had a 30% greater risk of dying. Some of the studies had serious flaws even beyond the one I've been describing here. When those particularly bad studies were set aside, the ratio decreased to 1.24, meaning that always-singles had a 24% greater risk of dying than those who got married and were currently married.

Considering that the number of people who married but got tossed out of the currently-married group (because they divorced or became widowed) may have approached 50% even without the widowed group, I'm not impressed. I think I'll hold off a bit before giving away all of my worldly goods.

All of the other analyses were based on all of the studies, not just the less-bad ones. That means that the reported death rates for singles are probably lower than the numbers suggest. Here are a few of the more specific findings:

- The relative risk of death was higher for single men (1.32) than single women (1.23).
- By region, singles relative mortality risk (hazard ratio) was highest for China, Japan, and Taiwan (1.94) and lowest for the British Commonwealth (1.14) and Bangladesh and Lebanon (1.12). For the U.S., it was 1.23.
- Singles' relative mortality risk was highest in studies of 30-39 year-olds (2.28), and decreased every decade thereafter. So, it was 1.80 for people in their 40s, 1.55 for people in their 50s, 1.28 for those in their 60s, and 1.16 for the 70-somethings. (Of course, in the very young groups, the overall death rates are very low.)
- "The relative mortality risk for singles has increased over the last few decades." Those are the authors' words. Looking at the results reported for each decade, though, what I see is this: **For studies that started in 1950 or earlier, the relative mortality risk was not significantly different for the currently married compared to the always-single. In fact, for studies that started between 1940 and 1949, the always-singles lived non-significantly longer** than those who were currently married when the study began. It is only in the studies that started in 1960 or later that singles have higher relative mortality ratios than the currently married. I have an idea about this finding that I'll come back to later.

When the authors get to the Discussion section, which is where authors are supposed to speculate about what it all means, they do make one point that does not amount to a whole lot of singlism and matrimania. They suggest that higher risk of health problems and early death may be tied to meager health benefits, stingy levels of public assistance, and shrinking wages. These kinds of financial challenges are likely to be even greater for singles than for the currently married (who, for example, may have access to health care through a spouse's plan if they don't have their own, and who may have two salaries to pay for one set of utility bills and one rent or mortgage).

As for the other explanations, hold your nose. Here's just one example of an idea they float for why the relative risk of mortality decreases with age: "it may be that as people age, they acclimate to being single, finding ways to compensate for the lack of instrumental and social support that are associated with being married." Yes, singles, let's all learn to "compensate" for the supposed voids in our lives. You will not be surprised to hear that the authors cite, uncritically, the Marriage Mafia's favorite source, Linda Waite and Maggie Gallagher's book that I took apart claim by claim in *Singled Out*. They do not cite the national surveys showing that always-single people are more likely than the currently married to visit, support, and maintain ties with their parents, siblings, friends, and neighbors.

In talking to the MSNBC reporter, the lead author of the "singles are doomed" study reiterates Waite and Gallagher's fantasies about married people eating better because they are married. (I mocked that here, with some dissenting data.) Of course, he doesn't mention the research on how getting married is also linked with getting fatter, which does not seem all that compatible with eating better.

There is so much to say about the results of this meta-analysis and the matrimaniacal interpretations offered by the authors, but I still think the most important point is that the always-single group includes all singles, whereas the currently-married group sets aside everyone who got married and then divorced. What we really need is a comparison between all people who stayed single and all of the people who ever got married. You won't find that comparison in this mortality meta-analysis.

So what's the closest thing you can find? Is there a group of people especially likely to stay married even if they are very unhappily married and perhaps, under other circumstances, would prefer to divorce? Here's my guess: That was the situation before the 1960s. For many people, divorce was just considered way too shameful, so miserable married couples just toughed it out. Remember the findings from the studies conducted before 1960? There were not that many of them, so caution is in order. Still, there were no significant differences in relative mortality rates for the currently married compared to the always-single.

Bottom Line

The meta-analysis showed that married people live longer than people who stay single, as long as you include everyone in the group of singles (whether they want to be single or not) but exclude from the group of people who got married anyone who hated their marriage and got divorced (as well as anyone who became widowed). This, of course, is the familiar cheater technique. It does not show that if you get married, you will live longer. It just pretends to do so when it is reported in sensationalized media scare stories.

So what about the fact that this meta-analysis was based on 90 studies and about 500 million people? Those are the sorts of numbers that are catnip for the practitioners of singlism. To those who care about good science and rigorous conclusions, they should be irrelevant. As long as the studies are based on the cheater technique of skimming off the top of the married group only those who stayed married, it doesn't matter if there were 90 studies or 900, 500 million people or 5 billion people. If you add one flawed study to another, you just get two flawed studies.

Suppose the research had been done in a way that did *not* give the married group a great big advantage over the single group. Say the researchers had compared all of the people who had ever married to all of the people who stayed single, and still found that the single group had a higher risk of mortality than the married group. Would that mean that the prediction of your premature demise was accurate?

It would be a stronger case, but I still would not jump off the nearest cliff to get this early death thing over with as soon as possible. The results of studies are about averages, not about specific individuals. There are always exceptions. Also, remember that people choose for themselves whether to marry. (In scientific studies where it is ethically feasible, you randomly assign people to different conditions - for example, the drug group vs. the placebo. You can't do that with marriage, single life, widowhood, and divorce.)

The kinds of people who choose to marry (or at least some of them) may be the kinds of people who do better as married people than they would as singles. Some of the people who choose to stay single may have healthier and longer lives than if they married. There is no research on the topic, but my guess is that for people who are single at heart, getting married would do them no good at all.

[**UPDATE**: Best headline so far about this whole bogus episode is from Jezebel: "A gentle reminder that being single will kill you"]

[Originally published at the "Living Single" blog at *Psychology Today* on August 18, 2011.]

PART IV

WHAT'S REALLY GOING ON HERE?

37

The Skeptical Reader: How the Media, and Even Academic Journals, Get Things Wrong

Sadly, social scientists often suspend their critical thinking when the topic is marriage

In the past two posts ([here] and [here]), I have been critiquing the latest study making claims about marital status and cancer survival rates. In this final post in the series, I will show you examples of how the *New York Times* and an editorial in an academic journal gave readers a misleading impression of what the study really did demonstrate.

Misleading Media Reports: The Example of the New York Times

Read any story about this study in the media and you can probably find lots of statements that give misleading impressions. I'm going to pick on the *New York Times*. In a [10-paragraph article], I had something skeptical to say about 8 of them.

> *"Married cancer patients live longer than single people who have the disease, suggesting that logistical and emotional support from a loved one may be far more critical to cancer care than previously recognized."*

Actually, we have no idea whether logistical or emotional support mattered. None of that was measured.

> *"Numerous studies have suggested that married people have better overall health than single people, but those data likely are skewed by the fact that healthy people are more likely to have opportunities to marry."*

That skewing is just one of the many problems with such research. Studies comparing the currently married to everyone else, and then making claims about causality, are making claims that are scientifically indefensible. If you want to claim that getting married makes you healthier, then you need to compare all of the people who ever got married to the people who stayed single. To claim that married people are healthier by doing research in which you set aside all the people who got married, hated it, and got divorced, is to engage in cheater science. If you wanted to make a claim about a new drug, you would not rely on studies which set aside all of the people who took it, hated it, and refused to continue taking it.

> *"'When you have a spouse who is present when the patient is diagnosed, they are an invested party and they are going to more than likely make sure the patient goes to the doctor, that they get the necessary treatments…'"*

That's an assumption. It was not demonstrated in the study. It may or may not be true.

"The study, <u>published in The Journal of Clinical Oncology</u>, found that single patients were 53 percent less likely to receive appropriate therapy than married patients. The finding suggests that maintaining grueling chemotherapy and radiation schedules and taking medication as prescribed is easier for people who have help from a spouse compared with single people who must manage the logistics of cancer treatment on their own."

The authors did not have any data on whether the single people had any help with logistics. The study did not include any measures of maintaining treatment schedules or taking medication. In fact, we do not even know whether doctors prescribed the same treatments to the single patients and the married patients. And if single patients had been prescribed the same treatments and did not make it through them all as often as married patients did, we don't know whether other factors may have been in play. For example, maybe the unmarried patients ran out of money sooner. Or maybe the unmarried patients were not treated as well as the married patients were (not just medically, but in other ways, too). Again, my claim is not that the proposed interpretation is wrong, but that we just don't know.

"Unmarried cancer patients also were 17 percent more likely to have late-stage cancer at the time of diagnosis, compared with married patients. That suggests that spouses play a role in encouraging patients to see a doctor, while single people may put off doctor visits, resulting in a more advanced cancer by the time they finally seek a diagnosis."

We don't know whether spouses played a role in encouraging patients to see a doctor. That was not assessed. Again, everyone is just guessing. All of these guesses could be right or they could be wrong – we just don't know.

"The data do not distinguish between same-sex and opposite-sex couples and don't account for patients who are engaged or living with a partner. Because some of the people labeled as single in the study probably have a committed partner, it's likely that the findings actually understate the scope of the problem for people who are truly coping with a cancer diagnosis on their own."

This is the typical <u>one-sided skepticism</u>. What about all of the married people who are living separately – perhaps about 7 percent of them?

"Notably, men with cancer showed a greater benefit from marriage than did women. That doesn't mean husbands are not supportive of wives, but instead suggests that single women do a better job of reaching out for social support than do single men, so the gap between single and married women with cancer is not as great as the gap between single and married men with cancer."

Maybe, but again, we don't know. Reaching out for social support wasn't measured. We're still just guessing.

"For doctors and hospitals, the data show that being single is an important risk factor for failing to comply with medical treatments..."

Actually, the data don't show that. This is an interpretation of the results, not a statement of the results. It could be true or it could be false.

The Embarrassing Editorial in the Journal of Clinical Oncology

In an editorial in the journal in which the study was published, the writer described the findings and then said that the data were "incontrovertible." That's just embarrassing. The study was not a true experiment. Any study with this design results in data that are open to question.

The editorial then goes on to claim that "strikingly, the benefits of marriage are comparable to or greater than anticancer treatment with chemotherapy." First, as I described in detail previously, we don't know if this study tells us anything about the supposed "benefits of marriage." It may be about differences in wealth or in access to health care or in values or in discriminatory practices that favor married patients over single ones.

Second, no data on chemotherapy were included in the research. The authors compared the magnitude of their own findings to the results of other studies in which the effectiveness of chemotherapy was assessed. They were different studies of different people. They may or may not be comparable.

Third, the supposed "benefits" of marriage were *not* "comparable to or greater than" chemo. For 4 of the 9 cancers that were included in the analyses, chemo was better; for the other 5, "marriage" was.

The editorial has a pity-the-poor-single-people sensibility. We single people are described as "socially disconnected," "socially isolated," and "alienated." We may also have "limited health literacy." The greater health outcomes that the writer attributes, without qualification, to marriage, is (in his mind) a testament to "the power of human attachment." Because how could single people ever have human attachments.

The writer's intent is positive. He wants to encourage more supportive health care for single people. He just goes about it in a way that makes my inner social scientist cringe.

One Good Thing

Several people who sent me links to media reports about this study were impressed by one thing that they noticed. When it came time to spell out the implications for single people, reporters did not say that they should just get married. In so refraining, they were following the lead of the study's authors, who ended their article by suggesting that what single people need is more social support, both from medical professionals and beyond.

[Originally published at the "Single at Heart" blog at *PsychCentral* on October 30, 2013.]

38

The Crisis in Squishy Science and Trouble for Journalists

What should we make of conflicting findings?

I should be embarrassed. I'm a social psychologist and my field seems to be in a heap of trouble these days. All of the squishy sciences are getting battered.

"Squishy" isn't an insult. To me, it is more of a term of endearment. I use it to refer to all of the sciences that try in some way to study humans. The first time I taught a course in introductory psychology, a group of chemistry majors sat in the second row and lobbed disdainful questions at me. I wanted to tell them that they had chosen an easy discipline. If they wanted a real challenge, they should try studying the kinds of subjects who think and plan and scheme and push back on people who try to figure them out.

The squishy sciences are great at generating findings that are exciting and counter-intuitive. Journalists love those results. The trouble is coming from the growing realization that the innovative discoveries can turn out to be all too wobbly. Other scientists fail to replicate them, or even worse, they produce results that are contradictory.

At the *Chronicle of Higher Education*, Tom Bartlett's article, "Power of Suggestion," led with this tease: "The amazing influence of unconscious cues is among the most fascinating discoveries of our time – that is, if it is true." David Freedman told a similar cautionary tale at the *Columbia Journalism Review* in "Survival of the Wrongest." His story explained "how personal-health journalism ignores the fundamental pitfalls baked into all scientific research and serves up a daily diet of unreliable information."

As ominous as all this sounds, I am not embarrassed. In fact, I am relieved. It is about time that all of us – squishy scientists, the journalists who write about squishy science, and all of our readers – face up to our formidable assignment. What should we make of the messiness of our enterprise?

I.   The Cacophony of Conflicting Findings

A thicket of contradictory findings can be exasperating. It can tempt suspicions of evil, self-serving, or at least careless scientists. Sometimes, those nefarious explanations are true. But it is possible to amass a messy-looking pile of scientific papers, even when everyone is a competent scientist conducting good research in good faith. Here are just two of the reasons that can happen.

#1 Humans are more complicated than cupcakes; studying them is, too.
Think about the process of preparing your favorite sweets – brownies, for example. They are just brownies, but they can be fickle. Leave them in the oven for just a few extra minutes, and instead of getting yummy, gooey treats, you have brownie rocks.

People are even more temperamental than brownies. Two experimenters in different labs may think they are replicating the essence of the experiment in question, but perhaps something else is different. Something they didn't think much about, that has unanticipated implications for the psychology of participants. It could be something subtle about the way the experimenter interacts with the participants, or the ways certain questions are asked, or differences in participants' expectations about who is observing them or who could learn about their responses, or… well, the possibilities are endless.

Freedman made a similar point in a discussion of confounding factors. Happily, many potential confounds can be eliminated or minimized by good research practices. For example, experimenters should remain unaware of which participants are in which conditions. In a study of dieting, for instance, experimenters can't be more supportive of the participants on the diet they believe in if they don't know which particular diet a participant is on.

#2 Even if a finding is true, it will not necessarily show up in every study.

Consider a fact from the world of baseball that we know to be true: Joe DiMaggio was a better hitter than his teammate, Jerry Coleman. DiMaggio's lifetime batting average was .325; Coleman's, .263. On any given day when both men were in the line-up, though, DiMaggio would not always get more hits than Coleman. Do those particular games undermine the conclusion that DiMaggio was the better hitter? I'd say no, because you need to consider the totality of their careers – all of the games they played.

I like to think of each baseball game as akin to an individual social science study. Studies comparing, say, one particular diet to another may sometimes show one diet winning, others times show the other diet winning, and still other times show no difference at all. What matters (if all of the studies are equally sound, methodologically) is the cumulative effect. If one diet really is superior to another, then the weight of the evidence – when the evidence derives from rigorous research – will support the superior diet. Freedman recognized this when he advised journalists, "Look at the preponderance of the evidence."

But what about the publication bias that Freedman mentions? Won't some studies get preferential treatment at the hands of eager editors? That may be so. Plus, studies that show no statistically significant differences rarely see the light of the published day. That raises the potential problem that readers are only getting to know about the studies that did show differences, while remaining oblivious to the stacks of unpublished studies showing no differences.

There is, though, a statistical way of addressing this "file drawer problem." Though the procedure is not flawless, it is possible to calculate the number of limp studies that would need to be lurking in people's file drawers in order to wipe out the cumulative effect of the known and published studies.

The need to establish the replicability of findings is becoming more widely recognized. One consequence is that there may also be more opportunities than there were in the past to pull those studies out of their dusty file drawers and make them readily available to others. Online sites, without the same costs as print journals, are especially promising. Some, such as the Open Science Framework and Psych File Drawer, are already in the works.

II.   Compounding the Problems: Emotional Investments and Thumbs on the Scale

In a telling passage, Freedman expresses his exasperation with all of the sets of sharply contradictory findings in personal-health research:

"To cite just a few examples out of thousands, studies have found that hormone-replacement therapy is safe and effective, and also that it is dangerous and ineffective; that virtually every vitamin supplement lowers the risk of various diseases, and also that they do nothing for these diseases; that low-carb, high-fat diets are the most effective way to lose weight, and that high-carb, low-fat diets are the most effective way to lose weight..."

As frustrating as these inconsistencies are, they are also graced by an appealing symmetry. Some scientists, and perhaps some science writers, are invested in the low-carb, high-fat diets, whereas others would like to rest their thumbs on the scales of the high-carb, low-fat diets. The two sides get to fight it out.

For more than a decade, I have been doing research and writing on a topic in which just about all of the emotional investment is on one side of the argument. I study marital status, with an emphasis on the single side of the equation. Just about all thumbs are coaxing the scales to tip toward marriage.

Are married scientists invested in demonstrating their own superiority? I'm not sure. But many other groups, including religious and political organizations, have a stake in the supposed advantages of marriage over single life, and some are well-funded and politically active.

The scientists, together with the activists, have been insisting that getting married results in lasting improvements in happiness and health and many other important outcomes. They have been at it for so long, and with so little critical scrutiny, that their conclusions have become part of the conventional wisdom.

Back when I was just practicing single life, rather than also studying it, I assumed that the empirical support for such conclusions was probably about as strong as it could be, considering the challenges of trying to investigate phenomena (staying single, getting married, getting unmarried) that cannot be controlled or manipulated in a laboratory.

When I first started reading the original research reports that were the basis of so many of the claims in the media, I was stunned. By their very design, the studies could not possibly support the headlines I was reading in the press. There was a causality implied in many of the claims (get married, be happier) that no study could ever demonstrate. Even if the methodological problems were not so glaring and the results could be believed, the findings were not nearly as strong or as consistent as cultural conversations would lead us to believe.

I spelled out the problems in detail in *Singled Out: How Singles Are Stereotyped, Stigmatized, and Ignored, and Still Live Happily Ever After* and in much of the writing I have done since then. But the marriage apologists are dug in, and they have emotional fervor and organizational clout behind them.

The replication problem in research on marital status is distinct: There is a widespread perception that "getting married makes people happier" (or healthier or sexier or more successful parents or any other positive outcome you want to posit) is a finding that has been successfully replicated many times over. In fact, such a finding has never has been definitively demonstrated – not even once – and it never will be. We cannot randomly assign people to get married, stay single, or get unmarried.

Because this very basic point is so often missed, even – sadly – by seasoned social scientists, I will write more about it in a separate piece. There, I will offer some advice to fellow researchers for describing their results more accurately, both in their academic writings and in their popular writings and conversations with journalists.

Here, I'll end with some advice for journalists. I'm not one, so I don't know if my suggestions are reasonable or if they would help. I'd love to hear from people in the know.

III.   **What's a Journalist to Do?**

I think there are some steps journalists can take to improve the accuracy of their social science and personal-health reporting.

#1 Become a Rigorous Methodological Thinker

With so many pressures on journalists to do good work with ever-diminishing resources and opportunities, I wish I did not want to suggest something that entails even more time and effort. Still, I'll say it: I think top-notch methodological training is a must. If it is not already a requirement in journalism programs, I think anyone who writes about social science or health research should take a graduate level course in research methodology or its equivalent. Research courses in psychology are most likely to cover the kinds of methodological issues that arise in studies of human behavior; or maybe I just think that because I am a social psychologist. In any case, journalists need to be astute methodological thinkers who know how to assess research, so they are not left merely to take the words of the people they interview.

#2 Read the Original Research Yourself Before Reading Other Descriptions of the Research and Before Conducting Any Interviews

Has a press release come across your screen announcing some intriguing research? Don't finish reading it. Go to the original study being touted, read it, and critique it. Then go back and finish reading the press release.

#3 Don't Print Press Releases

The most disheartening line in David Freedman's piece is the report of a finding I've long suspected. Referring to a study of 500 stories about health in major newspapers, Freedman noted:

"In the survey, 44 percent of the 256 staff journalists who responded said that their organizations at times base stories almost entirely on press releases. Studies by other researchers have come to similar conclusions."

Don't be part of the 44 percent. Read the study for yourself. Ask your own questions. Find your own sources.

#4 Ask How the Results of the New Study Fit into the Existing Literature

All too often, media reports seem to treat individual studies as entities existing apart from all of the other research. Ask questions such as: Are the results consistent with previous studies on the topic? If not, why should we believe these results instead? There may be a good reason. Find out.

#5 Keep Tabs on Original Sources

If you aren't already doing so, sign up for content alerts from the relevant journals. See what's really out there, as opposed to just what's getting promoted with press releases.

#6 Read Contrarians

Dip into the writings of social and health scientists who are not echoing the same lines as everyone else. Contrarians such as the Freakonomics guys won't always be right, but maybe they will stir things up a bit. Then, perhaps, the stories you write will sound less like everyone else's.

If you follow all of these guidelines, maybe your stories will also be more accurate than everyone else's.

[Originally published at the "Living Single" blog at *Psychology Today* on February 14, 2013.]

39

Marriage Wars: The Real Fight is Over Moral Superiority

Straight people's marriages are not threatened – their claim to moral superiority is

Have you seen the "Gathering Storm" ad? It is the latest from the anti-gay marriage machine. Set against a grey, lightening-pocked, ominous background, it begins with the words: "There's a storm gathering. The clouds are dark and the winds are strong and I am afraid." It continues with one person after another (actors, all) declaring that same-sex marriage advocates are a threat. "Those advocates want to change the way I live," says one.

The ad touched off a televised maelstrom, with pairs of pundits yelling at and over each other with arguments that go round and round and never seem to come to any sensible resolution. The key question that befuddles gays who want to marry, and straights who have no problem with that, is this: How can one person's marriage threaten another person's? How is that even possible or plausible?

As Mike Barnicle asked when he was guest hosting Hardball, "I still don't get it. How, you know, if the couple upstairs, Ray and Tommy - what do they have to do with my life downstairs?"

The predictable arguments are trotted out: God doesn't want it. Marriage is for procreation. It is the foundation of civilization. By now, all of these are high hanging curve balls for the batters on the other team who have been swinging away at these pitches for so long. (See, for example, this parody of the "Gathering Storm" ad, and this blog.)

Even if granted, though, none of the anti arguments answer that puzzling question - what does one person's marriage have to do with another person's? Just how, exactly, are gay marriage advocates going to "change the way [opponents] live?"

They aren't. But they are a threat nonetheless. If advocates were to succeed in achieving complete cultural and legal acceptance - maybe even celebration - of same-sex marriage, something truly significant would be lost by the other side. It is not something that those opponents can see or feel or hold in their hands, but they cling to it nonetheless. It is their view of the world.

Both sides have a worldview and wish fervently for theirs to prevail. Among some of those who oppose same-sex marriage, marriage really does have a sacred place. In their minds, it truly is the bedrock of civilization (anthropologists be damned!). Getting married is, to them personally, a transformative experience. It doesn't just make them more mature or more adult or just different from those who are not married - it makes them better.

That, I think, is the real reason why some (though not all) of the opponents of same-sex marriage are so vehement. It is why they feel so threatened. To open the door of marriage to gays is to let them in on the one resource that opponents are most reluctant to share (especially with gays) - their own sense of moral superiority.

The dark and scary motif of the gathering-storm ad aptly expresses a genuine sense of foreboding. Even though the arguments in the ad may be bogus, the fear is real.

If it really is a sense of moral superiority that is at stake, then it is also easy to understand the passion on the side of the advocates of gay marriage. The GLBT community has been so vilified for so long. They've been scorned as moral misfits. Now imagine if the mantle of marriage - the official, legal, federal, no-holds-barred kind - could confer instant respectability. No, not just respectability - superiority. MORAL superiority. Who wouldn't be tempted to reach for that diamond ring?

The marriage wars are not only about the moral high ground. I think there are sincerely-held motives on both sides that are worthy of respect. On the side of the opponents, they often are religious ones. On the side of the advocates, there is the wish to lean against that long arc, and bend it toward justice.

There are weighty practical matters as well, such as the 1,138 federal rights and protections afforded only to heterosexual married couples. The LGBT community is currently protesting their unequal opportunities in their very own tea party. The press release notes, for instance, that "LGBT individuals are blocked access to their partner's social security benefits, often making retirement financially difficult, if not impossible." The Family and Medical Leave Act (FMLA) is another example. Official marriage would mean that LGBT people could take time off under that policy to care for their partners.

I'd never stand in the way of non-discrimination, so same-sex marriage has my vote. Still, I don't like this route to fairness. Any attempt to achieve social justice simply by expanding membership in the Married Couples Club is always going to come up short. As a single person, I don't have access to anyone's social security benefits, and I can't leave my own for anyone else - they just go back into the system. Were I to fall ill, no one can take leave under FMLA to care for me, nor can I tap its protections in order to care for a peer who is especially important in my life. Where's the justice in that?

Fortunately, there is growing momentum for more inclusive approaches that do not make the marital door the sole point of access for caring, sharing, and fairness. The "Beyond Sane-Sex Marriage" project, Canada's "Beyond Conjugality" project, and Nancy Polikoff's *Beyond (Straight and Gay) Marriage* book are just a few of those efforts. Now there's a storm I'd like to gather in my arms and run with!

I started writing this post because Jen, a Living Single reader, asked whether I thought that people on both sides of the same-sex marriage debate were making arguments that are matrimaniacal. Were they, she wondered, viewing marriage as an all-purpose magical solution to everyone's problems? And, she asked, isn't all this incessant promotion of marriage, in a way, a devaluing of marriage?

I like Jen's questions. So much so, that I concluded the first chapter of *Singled Out* by raising just those sorts of issues:

> *This is not a book about the "plight" of singles as victims, but about their resilience. Obviously, I'm going to moan about the many ways that singles are viewed and treated unfairly. I've already started. But I will not end with the predictable "woe is us." Instead, I will express pride at how well so many singles do despite all the singlism and the matrimania. Singles, by definition, do not have that one special Sex and Everything Else Partner who is supposed to fill up all of their empty spaces with happiness, maturity, and meaning. Yet, as we will see, the singles who actually are miserable and immature and who believe their lives have no meaning are the exceptions. How can this be? And if married people so obviously have so much going for them, why do they need swarms of scientists, pundits, politicians, experts, authors, reporters, and entertainers making their case for them? (from p. 27 of Singled Out)*

> [Originally published at the "Living Single" blog at *Psychology Today* on April 12, 2009.]

40

The Topic that Turns Smart, Creative People into Mindless Spouters of Clichés

Even the most open-minded people can't help themselves: They are smug about marriage

Suppose I challenged you to write the most cliché-drenched ode to marriage you could possibly imagine. Don't do any critical thinking. Don't worry about whether what you have to say is true, or logically consistent, or whether it could be potentially offensive to millions, or whether it might serve as the basis for a women's studies essay on cultural criticism or a Saturday Night Live skit. Just pour it on thick.

Perhaps your essay would include excerpts such as the following:

- "There is tremendous social and spiritual value in marriage."
- Marriage "is transformative."
- When a man proposes to a woman, she looks at him with eyes that say, 'You're a real man."
- With marriage, you are "being propelled each day to fight the good fight it takes to provide for your family, rather than wanting to succeed because it boosts your ego, your status, and your self-image."
- Marriage is especially important for men: "There's just something about the right woman that helps you mature into that man you're supposed to be."
- "Marriage connects you to something bigger than yourself." For example, you no longer leave your socks on the floor and you learn to compromise.
- "Humans can't help but respect people for doing something that helps you perpetuate the human race."

The quotes you just read are real ones. They could easily have come straight from the mouths of right-wing ideologues such as Maggie Gallagher. No one would be surprised to find claims such as these at pro-marriage websites, including those excoriating same-sex marriage.

But no, the author of these marital bromides is Toure. He proudly read his mash-letter to marriage as part of the Daily Rant feature on the Dylan Ratigan Show, guest hosted that day by Matt Miller. You can listen to the entire rant here. Generate your own response, if you'd like. In my next post (the next and last chapter of this book), I'll explain what's wrong with the rant (in case that is not totally obvious) and why it made me mad and sad.

[Originally published at the "Single at Heart" blog at *PsychCentral* on March 7, 2012.]

41

A Rant about a Rant about Marriage

Some who rant about white privilege do not even recognize their marital privileges

In my previous post, The Topic that Turns Smart, Creative People into Mindless Spouters of Clichés, I quoted from Toure's ode to marriage in the "daily rant" feature of the Dylan Ratigan Show. Go ahead and read that first part, so you will have in mind the context for this post.

Here in Part 2, I will review just a few of the problems with Toure's platitudes.

Let's start with the one about how people who are married are "being propelled each day to fight the good fight it takes to provide for your family, rather than wanting to succeed because it boosts your ego, your status, and your self-image."

So those are my two choices? Either I'm providing for my family or I'm out to boost my ego, my status, and my self-image? Toure, there are around 100 million adults who are not married, and that's just counting the ones in the U.S. So Molly Ivins, Condoleezza Rice, Janet Napolitano, David Souter, Maggie Kuhn, Ralph Nader, every Pope, and all of the other lifelong singles were all out just to boost their egos? Consider, too, that many single people *are* providing for their family, including those who do not have children of their own. You have just insulted a whole lot of them. Plus, you do not flatter yourself by proposing this dopey dichotomy.

What about Toure's claim that by marrying, you help "perpetuate the human race"? Here I feel like Rachel Maddow explaining contraception to Mitt Romney, and that sort of naivete is not at all what I associated with Toure before I heard his rant. I feel embarrassed to spell this out but here goes: You don't need to be married to have kids.

Toure, do you really believe that it only occurs to married people to pick their socks up off the floor? And about needing to marry in order to learn to compromise, have you ever been in a workplace?

Now let's talk about the woman who looks at you with goo-goo eyes because you proposed to her, and only now believes that you have become a real man: That's kind of sad. And, in my opinion, bigoted. Single men are not fake men. And commitment comes in many varieties other than the marital kind.

I have a similar reaction to Toure's wistful reflection that "There's just something about the right woman that helps you mature into that man you're supposed to be." If a man can only mature with the help of the "right woman," I think that's a sorrowful statement about that man. I have much greater respect for the men who are all that they can be regardless of whether they ever marry.

Is marriage not just a valuable experience, but a "transformative" one? For more than a decade, the claim has been made that marrying transforms single people – otherwise doomed to nasty, brutish, and short lives – into blissfully happy, healthy, and long-living couples. When I wrote *Singled Out*, I looked up the data supposedly supporting such claims, and found it stunningly unconvincing. I still read closely just about every new journal article purporting to show the transformative power of marrying, and continue to be unimpressed.

In *Singled Out* (and in subsequent writings), I also took on Toure's belief that marriage is especially transformative for men, pushing and shoving them to, at last, grow up. That's a crock, too.

I will, though, grant Toure one way in which marrying really is transformative: It transforms single people from targets of unapologetic stereotyping and discrimination into privileged members of the Married Couples Club. It grants them the keys to the kingdom of presumptuousness. As long as you have that certificate, you are in. Regardless of the stuff you are made of, getting married means that you are "mature," "a real man," or a complete woman. No matter how insular and greedy your married life may actually be, you are pronounced "part of something bigger than yourself." You are, Toure maintains, a credit to your species.

There are plenty of people who glorify married people, and in the process, degrade single people – however unwittingly. I'm picking on Toure for a reason. He's smarter than that. He should know better. So should Matt Miller, the guest host who responded to Toure's rant by exclaiming, "Toure, I love that!" and "I agree with all of this."

Matt Miller, who also uncritically highlighted some singles-bashing during a previous stint as Dylan Ratigan's guest host, is, like Toure, not usually one to mindlessly parrot the conservative party line. Dylan Ratigan also fashions himself as a thinker, and often really is. But he, too, has been credulous about the links between marriage and happiness, and has reiterated such shaky statements with as much cautiousness as would Tony Perkins.

The stereotyping, stigmatizing, and discrimination against single people – what I call singlism – is pervasive. So is matrimania – the over-the-top hyping of weddings and marriage and coupling. What's more, singlism and matrimania slip by mostly unnoticed and unquestioned, even by progressives and by the intellectual vanguard of our society. That has to stop.

In the most recent issue of *Time* magazine, Toure contributed an essay on "Black Irony," one of the magazine's "Top 10 Ideas that Are Changing Your Life." (Living solo was #1.) In it, he said,

> "While our parents battled oppression, we're left to explain that racism is still present to skeptical people who continue to benefit from white privilege but struggle to see how."

Toure, I would like to explain that marital privilege is present and always has been, and that you are benefiting from it.

[Originally published at the "Single at Heart" blog at *PsychCentral* on March 7, 2012.]

ABOUT THE AUTHOR

Bella DePaulo (Ph.D., Harvard University) writes myth-busting, consciousness-raising, totally unapologetic books on single life. The *Atlantic* magazine has described her as "America's foremost thinker and writer on the single experience."

Dr. DePaulo's books get much attention because of her expertise, her high profile in the media, and her years of writing for popular audiences. Her work has been described in the most influential newspapers, including *New York Times* (many times), the *Washington Post*, the *Wall Street Journal*, and *USA Today*, and in widely-read magazines such as the *New Yorker*, *Time*, *AARP Magazine*, *Newsweek / The Daily Beast*, the *Week*, the *Economist*, *More*, *Glamour*, *Cosmopolitan*, *Elle*, *Readers' Digest*, *Prevention*, the *Nation*, *Business Week*, *US News & World Report*, *Realtor Magazine*, the *Chronicle of Higher Education*, and the *Atlantic*. Many newspapers and magazines around the world have also discussed her ideas. Bella DePaulo has been writing the "Living Single" blog for *Psychology Today* since 2008. She also blogs for PsychCentral and has contributed to the Huffington Post. She has appeared many times on radio and television, including, for example, NPR, *The Today Show*, *Good Morning America*, *NBC Nightly News*, *Hardball with Chris Matthews*, and *Anderson Cooper 360*.

Professor DePaulo, who is also an expert on the psychology of deceiving and detecting deceit, has lectured nationally and internationally. She has given workshops and has addressed criminal attorneys, judges, polygraphers, members of the national intelligence community (such as the CIA and the FBI), physicists, marketing professionals, high school teachers, and medical and mental health practitioners. She has been invited to speak at think tanks, government agencies, political meetings, singles advocacy groups, literary conferences, book clubs, book festivals, women's centers, newcomers groups, and many universities.

Bella DePaulo is the winner of the Excellence in Research Award, bestowed by the American Association for Single People. The author of more than 100 scholarly publications, including more than a dozen books, she has also won two prestigious academic awards, the Research Scientist Development Award and the James McKeen Cattell Award. Professor DePaulo has served in leadership positions in professional organizations and has served on the editorial boards of many journals. She is currently a Project Scientist in the psychology department at the University of California at Santa Barbara. Visit Dr. DePaulo's website at www.BellaDePaulo.com.